Margaret Junkin Preston

Poet of the Confederacy

Margaret Junkin Preston

POET OF THE CONFEDERACY

A Literary Life

STACEY JEAN KLEIN

The University of South Carolina Press

© 2007 University of South Carolina

Published by the University of South Carolina Press
Columbia, South Carolina 29208

www.sc.edu/uscpress

Manufactured in the United States of America

16 15 14 13 12 11 10 09 08 07   10 9 8 7 6 5 4 3 2 1

Library of Congress Cataloging-in-Publication Data

Klein, Stacey Jean, 1968–
    Margaret Junkin Preston, poet of the Confederacy : a literary life / Stacey Jean Klein.
        p. cm.
    Includes bibliographical references and index.
    ISBN-13: 978-1-57003-704-7 (cloth : alk. paper)
    ISBN-10: 1-57003-704-3 (cloth : alk. paper)
    1. Preston, Margaret Junkin, 1820–1897. 2. Women and literature—United States—
History—19th century. 3. Authors, American—19th century—Biography. 4. Women
and literature—Southern States. 5. Lexington (Va.)—Biography. I. Title.
    PS2663.K58 2007
    811'.4—dc22
    [B]   007007317

This book was printed on Glatfelter Natures, a recycled paper with 50 percent
postconsumer waste content.

For my mother, Donna Jean,
my grandmother Sarah Elizabeth,
and my great-grandmother Vella Belle:
three beautiful Southern women

and for David Christopher

CONTENTS

ILLUSTRATIONS

Preface

Margaret Junkin Preston's name came to my attention at several stages of my graduate career. I first became interested in the impact of the Civil War on Southern women while pursuing my master's degree at the University of South Carolina, and I found Preston's eloquent diary recounting her wartime experiences. While working toward my doctoral degree at the University of Illinois, I developed an interest in the cultural life of the nineteenth-century South, and Preston emerged as a central figure. A few years later, I became fascinated by the stories of families divided by the Civil War, and I discovered Preston once again. It seemed obvious that I should study this important and largely forgotten woman.

Though Preston's story touches on many of the threads of nineteenth-century U.S. history I find most interesting, its greatest value lies in explaining the expansion of white woman's place in the South. The Civil War was the greatest catalyst for change in Preston's life, just as I believe it was for most, if not all, Southern women of the nineteenth century. Preston's story suggests answers for many of the questions historians have asked about Southern women in recent years, and it is my hope that her experiences will be compared to those of other women. When these comparisons are made, I believe Preston's journey will prove to be typical rather than exceptional.

I also hope to resurrect the name of a woman for whom I have developed much respect and appreciation. In 1888 the *Washington Post* called Preston "one of the really famous American authors of the day." Yet she has been almost entirely forgotten. When she is remembered, as she has been by a few recent scholars, she is misunderstood and misrepresented. Preston was too important in her own time—and is too significant to our historical understanding—for this neglect to continue.

In the mid-1850s Margaret Junkin described the social barriers she and others like her faced: "But what business has a *woman* with authorship? Is she not looked upon as an intruder in the field of literary labor? Is she not constantly reminded that *home* is her province, and that her utmost ambition should extend no farther than to dress the garden of *man*'s heart and plant affections there? She must content herself with this sphere, nor ever venture out, Ruth-like, to glean behind the reapers."[1] Shortly after she wrote these lines, following nearly a decade of unsuccessfully challenging the barriers she described, Junkin stopped publishing altogether. Yet a few years later, with the married name of Margaret Preston, she became one of the South's most respected authors, a distinction she maintained until her death in 1897. What accounts for the dramatic improvement in Preston's fortunes? It was the Civil War that changed everything. During the war Preston and other women writers in the South found new methods by which to gain acceptance. In the later decades of the nineteenth century they maintained the expanded boundaries they had created during the war.

The life and career of Margaret Junkin Preston provide an example of how these women used the Civil War to increase woman's presence on the Southern cultural landscape both during and after the conflict. By finding a point at which their needs converged with those of the Confederacy, and later the postwar South, they expanded the place of Southern white women in the nineteenth century. Of course, they paid a price for their achievements, and compromises had to be made. But their accomplishments were unmistakable.

This study of Margaret Junkin Preston builds on recent historical scholarship concerning white woman's place in the nineteenth-century South and the effect the Civil War had on that place. Margaret Junkin moved from Pennsylvania to Lexington, Virginia, when she was twenty-eight years old, still unmarried and already a published author. She faced greater barriers than she had known in the North, and her willingness to challenge those limits through her writing has left us with a rich and nuanced description of white woman's place in the antebellum South. This description expands on the important work of such historians as Elizabeth Fox-Genovese. In *Within the Plantation Household: Black and White Women of the Old South* (1988) Fox-Genovese argues that gender relations—"the relations between women and men within specific societies and communities"—constitute the foundation of any society. Gender relations differ among various societies, but all societies tend to "promote distinct roles for women and men." Within these gender roles women and men form their sense of identity.[2]

The dominant gender relations in antebellum Southern society, according to Fox-Genovese, formed a "system of conventions that guided women's behavior and identities." These gender conventions limited the Southern woman's freedom to live her life as she chose. Fox-Genovese maintains that Southerners of all classes believed there were defined places for women and men. Women were to be subordinate to men, their place was the domestic—the family and the household. There, they would be governed and protected by men. Men represented their families and households in public places, such as the political world. It was unusual for a white woman not to have this protection, for Southern women married by their early twenties at the latest. There were fewer single women in the South—and fewer opportunities for them—than there were in the northern United States or in Europe. According to Fox-Genovese, never-married women faced "personal loneliness" and were social anomalies.[3]

One significant antebellum gender convention was the prohibition against female authorship. Fox-Genovese writes that publication was considered to be "unladylike self-display."[4] This attitude was present in the North also, but by the 1850s Northern women writers had slowly developed a distinct literary culture, staying within the confines of their assigned gender roles. Even by these standards, according to Fox-Genovese, Southern women were slow to take up their pens. If they challenged their place by publishing, they normally represented women in conformity with the existing social order. Rarely, Fox-Genovese argues, did white women reject the system of relations in the South. Yet Junkin fought against it for nearly a decade, using her pen as her weapon. In protesting against white woman's place in the Old South, Junkin described that place and all its complexities. Her words add to our understanding of the gender roles, relations, and identities Fox-Genovese outlines. The fact that Junkin capitulated in fewer than ten years—and grudgingly accepted an identity thrust on her by her new society—testifies to the strength of Southern gender conventions.

Margaret Junkin Preston's success in challenging those conventions during and after the Civil War tells us much about the effects of the war on Southern white woman's place. This topic has been examined by scholars such as George Rable. His *Civil Wars: Women and the Crisis of Southern Nationalism* (1989) explores how white women reacted to their societally imposed place and how the war changed women's social identity. Rable agrees with Fox-Genovese that white women in the antebellum South rarely challenged their society's assumptions about their proper role. The war, according to Rable, forced women to behave in untraditional ways. They managed plantations, volunteered in hospitals, and worked as nurses, teachers, and government clerks. Yet, even as gender roles were being violated, Rable maintains that "an essential conservatism" prevailed. Southerners understood that these changes were temporary; they came with the war and would be forgotten after the peace. During Reconstruction a "reactionary climate" took hold, and white Southern men and women reestablished proper gender roles. The traditional definition of woman's place survived, and women's destiny remained tied to the domestic circle. Rable acknowledges that there were some signs of change in the postwar South, since the war had demonstrated women were capable of mental and physical exertion. But he stresses that "ideological flexibility should not be confused with meaningful social change."[5] Rable briefly mentions the increased numbers of women writers after the war, but he fails to explain what we are to make of this phenomenon.

He neither challenges Fox-Genovese's argument that they crossed gender barriers, nor does he maintain that they were exceptions to his rule.

In *Mothers of Invention: Women of the Slaveholding South in the American Civil War* (1996) Drew Faust covers some of the same ground as Rable; yet Faust's interpretations are somewhat different. She agrees with Rable that after the war upper-class white women clung to traditional notions of patriarchy. Yet at the same time they began to define and defend their own interests as never before. Therefore, they invented "new selves erected firmly upon the elitist assumptions of the old." The war, according to Faust, inaugurated a reconsideration of traditional gender roles in the South and generated uncertainty about gender identities. Faust discusses the new responsibilities white women fulfilled during the war. But she believes that, far more important than what women did, was what men failed to do. White upper-class women, Faust argues, accepted subordination to men in exchange for protection and support. When men did not keep their end of this bargain, which seemed increasingly to be the case during the war, women developed a new sense of self. They became more aware of their needs, interests, and rights, rather than just their duties and obligations. As this self-awareness grew, white women's support of the war waned. Postwar women hoped they could rely on the men in their lives, but experience had taught them they needed to protect their own interests.[6]

Both Faust and Rable point to white women's contributions to the cult of the "Lost Cause"—the perpetuation and preservation of an idealized vision of the Old South and the Confederacy—as evidence that these women were rehabilitating traditional gender roles. Margaret Preston, through her writing, contributed to the Lost Cause on several occasions. Her motives, however, were decidedly different from those described by Faust and Rable. She was partly motivated by her love of her adopted region and her sorrow at its defeat. Yet she was also driven by her desire to continue the career she had revived during the war. She had learned that she could be accepted as a publishing author if her writing served a public purpose. After the war the cult of the Lost Cause was an obvious direction in which to take her career. She therefore used a seemingly traditional vehicle to achieve nontraditional results. This proved to be a recurring theme throughout Preston's post-1848 career: she hid her agenda behind a conservative facade.

Margaret Junkin Preston's story tells us that the Civil War did provide the means for women to expand their place positively and permanently, for they learned that their writing was accepted if it served the public. The public cause that allowed Preston to rejuvenate her writing career and find acceptance as a publishing female author in the South was Confederate nationalism. Recent scholarship by Catherine Clinton has begun to address the effects of Confederate nationalism on Southern white woman's place. In *Tara Revisited: Women,*

War, and the Plantation Legend (1995) Clinton writes, "The emergence of Confederate nationalism offered Southern ladies unprecedented opportunities to serve." While women's voluntary movements flourished in the antebellum North, such activity was discouraged in the South, so concerned was the region that women stay in the protected domestic sphere. Yet, with the coming of the war, white women were not only allowed to shift their interests from the private to the public, they were expected to do so. Their labors were needed to serve the new nation and its cause. Naturally many women performed services in keeping with their prescribed roles: sewing uniforms, knitting socks, rolling bandages. Yet some women stepped far from their traditional place, working as the nurses and clerks whom Rable also discusses, and even serving as spies, smugglers, and soldiers. (This last category required women to pose as men.) While Clinton does not address the cultural life of the Confederacy, this work will argue that women also served the new nation by contributing to its literature.[7]

There have been many excellent studies of nineteenth-century women writers in the United States—by scholars such as Nina Baym, Susan Coultrap-McQuin, Mary Kelley, and Elizabeth Moss. All have added to our understanding of these writers, their works, and the conditions under which they wrote. More recently, Karen L. Cox and Sarah E. Gardner have argued that women writers in the South did much more to shape the cultural and political climate of their region than has been previously understood. Yet none of these works has examined the degree to which women used their writing to better their own condition.[8]

This multidimensional biographical study of Margaret Junkin Preston will further our understanding of white woman's place in the Old South and what women did with that place during and after the war. Historians, including Faust and Rable, have recognized Preston's relevance to their projects, but the context of her life and work is necessary in order to understand her significance. In *Civil Wars* Rable quotes one of Preston's letters to the well-known Southern author Paul Hamilton Hayne: "I scorn to see a woman, who confesses even to very positive literary proclivities, turn with contempt from, or neglect the proper performance of a single woman's household duties." Rable then asks how much frustration and private rebellion these remarks masked. The following pages will make clear that Preston's frustration with, and rebellion against, woman's duties was rather public. She made statements such as this as part of the conservative facade she employed. Rable goes on to imply that Preston "labor[ed] in obscurity" after the war. While largely forgotten today, she was in fact one of the best-known authors in the South, if not in the United States.[9]

In *Mothers of Invention* Drew Faust points to Preston as an example of a woman whose support of the war faded the more she was called on to sacrifice. She quotes Preston's diary: "Who thinks or cares for victory now!"[10] But this statement was made on September 6, 1862, fairly early in the conflict. Preston's path was actually opposite to the one Faust describes in *Mothers of Invention* and similar to the one William Blair outlines in *Virginia's Private War: Feeding Body and Soul in the Confederacy, 1861–1865* (1998).[11] Preston was initially deeply divided by a conflict that pitted her homeland against her adopted land. Trying circumstances increased her support of the Confederacy, especially Union general David Hunter's invasion of Lexington in June 1864. By war's end Preston identified herself as a Confederate and wished for the South never to surrender, no matter the cost.

Two previous works have been written about Preston. The first, *The Life and Letters of Margaret Junkin Preston* (1903) is by her stepdaughter, Elizabeth Preston Allan. Allan's book provides some basic biographical information as well as valuable family anecdotes. It also includes approximately thirty letters to and from Preston, as well as Preston's wartime diary, kept between April 1862 and July 1865. The second, Mary Price Coulling's *Margaret Junkin Preston: A Biography* (1993), adds to our understanding of Preston's personal relations. I am deeply indebted to both authors for their efforts.[12]

Acknowledgments

I have been aided in this quest by several notable individuals. This book might not exist without the consistent encouragement and advice of Walter L. Arnstein. One would be hard pressed to find any adviser as helpful, much less one whose primary field of study is not even on the same continent. I count Professor Arnstein and his wife, Charlotte, as dear friends; they have always opened their home and their hearts to me. John H. Pruett is a true Southern gentleman in every sense of the word. I count him now as a friend as well as a mentor. It was my major adviser, Robert W. Johannsen, who first suggested that I dedicate a project entirely to Preston. It was also he who took me under his wing at the start of my graduate career. I will always be grateful.

An earlier version of chapter 5 in this book appeared as an article in the September 2003 issue of *Civil War History,* and I thank that journal for permission to include some of that material here. Though I am a recent entrant in the world of book publishing, I know that the University of South Carolina Press has been especially kind. In particular I wish to thank Alex Moore, who was the first to decide that Margaret Preston deserved some attention.

Chapter One

LESSONS LEARNED

Early Years, 1820–1832

Considering her importance to the history of Southern women, Margaret Junkin's story begins in an unlikely place. She was born in Milton, Pennsylvania, on May 19, 1820, the first child of the Reverend George Junkin and his wife, Julia. Milton, a river village in the center of the state, was the site of George Junkin's first and only pastorate in the Associate Reformed Presbyterian Church. The Junkins were devout members of the church, a more conservative offshoot of traditional Presbyterianism.[1]

Margaret Junkin's ancestry through both her parents was Scottish. Her mother, Julia Rush Miller, was the daughter of Scottish immigrants and enjoyed a relatively privileged upbringing in Philadelphia. John Miller, Margaret Junkin's maternal grandfather, was a successful marble worker and stonemason. Through his profession, the Millers had become friends with such notable individuals as Benjamin Rush, a prominent physician and signer of the Declaration of Independence. In fact Julia Miller was named for Dr. Rush's wife. The Millers were members of the Presbyterian Church at Germantown, a community near Philadelphia, and eventually John Miller became a ruling elder of that church.[2]

Margaret Junkin's ancestors, according to family legend, had moved from Inverness, Scotland, to County Antrim, Ireland, to escape persecution by the Stuarts.[3] Joseph Junkin, her great-grandfather, moved to Pennsylvania from Ireland around 1735.[4] His wife, Elizabeth, also according to legend, had as a child been in the siege of Londonderry (1689–1690), in which Protestant defenders held off Catholic forces for more than one hundred days. Margaret Junkin was thus "brought up on tales of heroism for conscience' sake," according to her stepdaughter.[5]

Junkin heard additional stories of heroism in the family lore about her paternal grandfather, Joseph Junkin, Jr., son of Joseph and Elizabeth. Joseph, Jr., she was told, had served with Marie-Joseph du Motier, Marquis de Lafayette, at the Battle of Brandywine Creek (1777), a clash in which the patriots were unsuccessful in keeping the British from occupying Philadelphia.[6] The tales of her ancestors' persecution by the Stuarts, coupled with her grandfather's participation in the Revolution, taught young Margaret Junkin that Great Britain was the traditional enemy. Her father, George Junkin, was stoutly pro-Union throughout his lifetime, largely as a result of his father's firsthand knowledge of the struggle to make that Union.[7]

George Junkin, the sixth child of Joseph, Jr., and Eleanor Cochrane, was born on November 1, 1790, in what is now Cumberland County, Pennsylvania. Eventually eight more children joined the household.[8] Receiving his early education in the log schoolhouses of the frontier, George graduated in 1813 from Jefferson College at Canonsburg, Pennsylvania. He immediately began studying for the ministry under the Reverend John Mitchell Mason, an eminent Presbyterian theologian in New York City. George was licensed to preach by the Associate Reformed Presbytery of Monongahela in 1816 and ordained by the Associate Reformed Presbytery of Philadelphia almost two years later.[9] George Junkin and Julia Rush Miller were wed in Philadelphia on June 1, 1819. The Reverend Junkin was installed in his pastorate at Milton on October 17 of that same year.[10]

George Junkin was without a doubt the single most important influence in his daughter's life. He was a man with strong beliefs, and he communicated those beliefs to the public throughout his lifetime in sermons, speeches, newspaper articles, and books. (All will be discussed in this book.) Most dear to the Reverend Junkin were his religious tenets. George Junkin was a strict Calvinist, and he believed in the concepts of human depravity and predestination. In his work *A Treatise on Justification* (second edition, 1849) he explained that all people, even infants, are sinful because of Adam's fall. Because they are too depraved to restore themselves to God, he believed, an individual must remain in spiritual darkness until God gives him light, thereby destining him for salvation.[11]

The Reverend Junkin held fast to these grim beliefs, despite the rising tide against them. As he and his wife started their family, the series of religious revivals known as the Second Great Awakening was sweeping the new nation. Preachers in this movement stressed that human beings had a role and a choice in their own salvation. This modern religious philosophy dovetailed nicely with the nation's burgeoning faith in democracy.[12] But George Junkin refused to be swayed, and he played a key role in the struggle between old and new that soon enveloped the Presbyterian Church.

As she grew older, Margaret Junkin was exposed to the new currents in religious thought, but when she was a small child, her father's stern philosophy prevailed. One Sunday afternoon during her childhood, Junkin, who was small for her age, with abundant curls and blue eyes, was playing outside. A theological student, displeased with her behavior on the sabbath, took her to a darkened room, where he questioned her about the safety of her soul. The student was evidently not satisfied with the little girl's answers, because he told her that he was afraid her soul was going to be lost. Junkin took the matter very seriously, and the young girl who had been playing childhood games just moments earlier began to worry whether or not she had received God's grace. In fact she was so haunted by the experience that her children noticed her as a grown woman "shiver[ing] at the recollection." She was glad, she told them, that they had been raised to believe in a more loving God.[13]

George Junkin brought another serious subject into his daughter's life while she was still very young. As a girl of six, she had no experience with, or understanding of, the concept of death. One day her father asked her to accompany him on a carriage ride. Margaret Junkin enjoyed herself until the carriage pulled up to a neighbor's house. Being a shy little girl, she was frightened to see "the shady front yard filled with people," Junkin recalled sixty-five years later. The young child's fear was elevated when her father took her inside the home and she found it darkened. Confused as to what had become of the joy she had experienced on her carriage ride, Junkin was lifted up by her father. She peered into what she later understood to be a coffin and saw the lifeless face of a fifteen-year-old boy whom she had seen alive just days before. George Junkin then took his daughter's hand and placed it on the dead boy's face. It was a terrifying introduction to death, one for which Margaret Junkin was completely unprepared.[14]

Junkin's terror was compounded by her inability to share her feelings with anyone, even her parents. Her father seemed unaware of the horrible effect the experience had on the little girl, and when she arrived home, she said nothing to her mother. Instead, in a pattern she followed throughout her life, she withdrew. The six-year-old child hid the "torturing memory," as she later called it, within herself. That night she lay awake trembling. "The fearful idea of death was borne into my soul," Junkin wrote many years later.[15]

George Junkin's attempts to provide his daughter with a superior education were far more successful. In nineteenth-century America the development of female minds was not taken seriously, for women were not expected to work outside the home.[16] A woman's identity was mostly encompassed in marriage, and the education of young girls therefore stressed the skills they needed to be wives and mothers. In fact, if a woman was too intellectual, she was often seen as unfeminine. This perception deterred many suitors, thus making it difficult for a woman to fulfill her ultimate purpose—marriage and motherhood.[17] Yet the Reverend Junkin placed greater value on Margaret's education than on notions of woman's proper place. Perhaps his reasons lay in his respect for knowledge and learning or in how impressed he became with his eldest daughter's intellectual capabilities. Indeed George Junkin apparently pushed Margaret further than he did any of his other children, including his sons. After Margaret's birth, the Junkin family had quickly expanded. While the family lived in Milton, five more children were born: John when Margaret was two years old; Joseph one year later; Eleanor in 1825; George, Jr., in 1827; and Ebenezer two years after George. All the Junkin children were first taught at home by their mother, who had received the best education afforded a girl in Philadelphia. The boys then attended local schools while the girls remained at home for instruction from their father. Margaret Junkin, scholarly and gifted in language, resembled her father intellectually more than did any of her siblings, and the Reverend Junkin taught her as much as she could absorb.[18] Consequently she received an education comparable to that received by boys her age.[19] She learned the Greek alphabet when she was just six years old. A devoted student, Junkin studied by candlelight after the rest of the family had gone to bed. Years later she told her children that her mother often admonished her to put out her candle. "It was the only respect in which I disobeyed my mother's wishes," Junkin told her stepdaughter, "and as my father encouraged my undertaking more than I could possibly do in the daytime, I felt justified." Junkin rose early and recited her lessons to her father before breakfast, again by candlelight. Soon she was reading texts in both Greek and Latin.[20]

While Margaret Junkin's education was expanding her mind, she was nevertheless learning that, because she was a female, her work was confined to the home. As soon as they could walk, the Junkin children were given chores. The boys worked outside in the fields and in the barn while the two girls stayed inside, helping their mother with the family cooking, washing, and sewing. Margaret Junkin later recalled that she, Eleanor, and their mother made everything that the family wore, even hand embroidering collars and cuffs.[21] The two little girls did find time to venture outdoors, where they played together. They developed a very close bond, largely because of their shared experiences.[22]

In June 1830, when Junkin was ten years old, the family moved from Milton to Germantown, where George Junkin had accepted the presidency of the Manual Labor Academy. The academy had been founded by Philadelphia Presbyterians in order to educate young men for the Christian ministry. According to the founders' plan, the students were to receive training in certain manual skills as well as in theology. They could then produce goods to be sold, defraying part of the cost of their education. In this way the ministry could be opened up to a greater number of young men. The idea appealed to the Reverend Junkin, and he left the pastoral ministry and moved his family east.[23]

The move to Germantown brought several positive changes into Margaret Junkin's life. The school's academic staff provided her with tutors in addition to her father. The most important of these was Charles F. McCay. McCay, like

George Junkin, was a graduate of Jefferson College. He was also ten years older than Margaret Junkin, and it was a testament to the young girl's maturity that he became her friend as well as her mentor.[24] Junkin was also now closer to her widowed grandmother, Margaret Miller, for whom she had been named. Margaret Miller spent a great deal of her time with one of her daughters in Oxford, Pennsylvania, a few hours' trip from Germantown. The two Margarets took walks in the countryside and spent evenings together around the fire, where the elder Margaret regaled her namesake with stories from her childhood in Scotland, as well as with Highland folklore. Mrs. Miller was probably the source of a story that Margaret Junkin told throughout her life, a Scottish legend concerning individuals of short stature. Junkin, who, as a grown woman, stood about five feet tall, told friends that she had been tossed on the horns of a cow as a child, an incident sure to stunt one's growth.[25]

Junkin found intellectual and personal happiness in Germantown, but her stay there was short-lived. The academy was suffering financially, and George Junkin was using his own money to keep it afloat. However, what brought an end to the Reverend Junkin's tenure as president was a controversy within the Presbyterian Church.[26] In 1822 the General Synod of the Associate Reformed Presbyterian Church united with the General Assembly of the Presbyterian Church. A few years later, in 1826, George Junkin was sent as a commissioner to the General Assembly and became prominent in the denomination's councils.[27] Around this time, tensions began to mount within the church. The trouble soon materialized into a conflict between two groups, known as the Old School and the New School. Old School followers, including the Reverend Junkin, held fast to the conservative, Calvinistic doctrines of predestination and human depravity.[28] New School followers were influenced by the teachings of the Second Great Awakening, believing man could contribute to his own salvation.[29]

The division within the Presbyterian Church came to a head with the controversy surrounding the Reverend Albert Barnes. Barnes, a respected pastor and theologian, was a graduate of Princeton Seminary. In 1829 he published a sermon, *The Way of Salvation,* which was critical of strict Calvinism. Shortly thereafter, when Barnes became pastor of the First Presbyterian Church of Philadelphia, conservatives within the Presbyterian Church charged him with heresy. In 1831 the case was brought before the General Assembly, where a New School majority ruled in Barnes's favor.[30]

Yet the Barnes saga was far from over. In 1835 Barnes restated his beliefs in *Notes on the Epistle to the Romans,* the first volume of his *Notes, Explanatory and Practical, on the Scriptures.*[31] The conservatives again brought charges, and, in the summer of 1835 Barnes was acquitted by the Second Presbytery of Philadelphia. George Junkin appealed this ruling and brought charges of heresy before the Synod of Philadelphia. The trial of the Reverend Albert Barnes in October

1835 received nationwide attention. The trial was not aimed at Barnes personally but rather at his views, which were shared by a large number of Presbyterians.[32] It was a battle between the Old School and the New School for control
of the church. During the trial George Junkin attacked Barnes's belief that individuals are sinners only because of the sins they commit themselves. He reem-
phasized Calvin's teaching that all are born with Adam's sin. This time the Old
School prevailed, and Barnes was suspended from the ministry until he re-
tracted his statements and repented.[33] Yet the conflict between the Old and New
Schools remained unresolved, and Barnes was restored to his pulpit by the General Assembly the next year.[34]

Even before the controversy over Albert Barnes had reached its ultimate conclusion, it had cost George Junkin his position at the Manual Labor Academy.
Most of the trustees at the academy were members of the New School, and they
were offended by the Reverend Junkin's attacks on Barnes. Therefore, in January 1832, when George Junkin heard that a college in Easton, Pennsylvania, was
searching for a president, he became interested in making a change. He accepted
the presidency of Lafayette College on the condition that the school adopt the
manual labor system. Soon thereafter, the Junkin family, including its newest
addition, William, left Germantown. Most of the students and faculty of the
Manual Labor Academy accompanied the Junkins to Easton, ending the life of
that institution.[35] For Margaret Junkin the move was especially painful. She
could not have known that Easton would prove to be an ideal place for her to
flourish both personally and intellectually. She knew only that she hated to leave
her grandmother and the cultural stimulus of nearby Philadelphia.[36] It was the
first time that her father's unyielding principles had altered her world, but it was
not the last.

Margaret Junkin Preston was a well-established author by the time this photograph was taken. Michael Miley Photograph Collection, Special Collections, Leyburn Library, Washington and Lee University, Lexington, Virginia. Courtesy of the Virginia Historical Society

George Junkin, an esteemed clergyman and educator, was the most important influence in the first half of his daughter's life. Washington and Lee Photograph Collection, Special Collections, Leyburn Library, Washington and Lee University, Lexington, Virginia

When Margaret Junkin married John Preston and moved into this house in Lexington, Virginia, she became the primary caregiver for six of his children. Two of those children, Elizabeth and John, are in the right foreground of the photograph. Rockbridge Historical Society Photograph Collection, Special Collections, Leyburn Library, Washington and Lee University, Lexington, Virginia

Elizabeth Preston Allan, the stepchild to whom Margaret Preston was closest, was also her first biographer. Michael Miley Photograph Collection, Special Collections, Leyburn Library, Washington and Lee University, Lexington, Virginia. Courtesy of the Virginia Historical Society

This photograph of Margaret Junkin Preston was taken in 1882, fifteen years before her death. Michael Miley Photograph Collection, Special Collections, Leyburn Library, Washington and Lee University, Lexington, Virginia. Courtesy of the Virginia Historical Society

AN AMERICAN FEMALE POET

Becoming a Published Author, 1832–1848

Margaret Junkin's new home did not boast the same cultural offerings as Germantown, but it was an attractive town, located at the confluence of the Lehigh and Delaware rivers. Easton had been laid out in 1750 according to the instructions of Thomas Penn, the son of Pennsylvania's founder. Its population in 1832 was roughly 3,700. There were five to six hundred houses in the town, thirty-three retail stores, and five weekly newspapers. Of the five churches in Easton, three were English speaking and two conducted services in German as well as in English.[1]

When the Junkin family arrived in Easton in March 1832, Lafayette College consisted only of a charter, which had been granted on March 9, 1826, and a board of trustees.[2] Under the guidance of George Junkin the college became a reality.[3] The Reverend Junkin had already insisted that the school follow the manual labor system, rather than proceed with plans to become a military college. Now, he set about proving the honor of manual labor. The president and his family worked side by side with the students and faculty constructing a permanent school building.[4]

The first classes at Lafayette College were held on May 9, 1832, with all recitations heard in one room. The original faculty of the college consisted of two people: Charles F. McCay, Margaret Junkin's friend and tutor from Germantown, and James I. Coon, also from the Manual Labor College. Like George Junkin and McCay, Coon, who taught classics at Lafayette, was a graduate of Jefferson College. McCay was the professor of mathematics and natural philosophy. As president, George Junkin nurtured the college's spiritual life, teaching a course once a week on the religion of the Bible and requiring that students attend prayers at five o'clock in the morning every day. All students were invited

to the Reverend Junkin's daily family devotions, and about half chose to partici-
pate.[5]

The formal inauguration of the president and faculty took place on May 1,
1834. In his inaugural address George Junkin explained his belief that religion
and education must be combined. Now Dr. Junkin after receiving an honorary
Doctor of Divinity degree from Jefferson College in 1833, he posed the following rhetorical questions: "Where is the church in whose vicinity no school is
taught? Where is the Christian sincere and true who opposes education? What
nation ever sunk in the scale of intelligence as she arose in Christian attain-
ments?"[6]

Yet George Junkin's steadfast devotion to his particular religious views soon
cost him many supporters, just as it had in Germantown. Enrollment dropped
for the 1837–38 school year, partly because of his involvement in the Albert
Barnes trial. Dr. Junkin had developed a reputation for having a stern and rigid
set of beliefs, and it did not help matters that this reputation was combined with
a serious demeanor. Dr. Samuel Gross, a well-known surgeon who was connected with Lafayette College during its early years, included his impressions of
George Junkin in his autobiography: "Dr. Junkin was an unpopular officer, a
Presbyterian preacher of the 'Old School,' and a man who, as he walked along,
never took his eyes off the ground, being evidently lost in deep thought, and,
consequently in no condition to notice anyone—student, friend, or citizen. Of
native kindness he had an abundance; he was a good disciplinarian, and was
regarded by many as a strong man in the pulpit for his argumentative powers
and the depth of his reasoning. His sermons, however, were always very long,
and therefore unpopular, especially with young persons."[7]

George Junkin may not have been entirely popular in Easton, but his oldest
daughter quickly made a niche for herself there. Margaret Junkin found that her
intellectual development was stimulated by the academic atmosphere, just as it
had been in Germantown. Her favorite tutor, Charles McCay, was there, and she
studied with other members of the faculty as well. Junkin also formed close
friendships with several of the school's undergraduates.[8] She was developing
into an industrious young lady. In addition to completing her own studies, she
helped with the education and the care of her siblings. "To all of us 'Maggie,' as
we always called her, was a little mother," Junkin's brother George later recalled.
"She ever had the most watchful care of us all, doing what she could to relieve
her parents, as to our physical well being, and especially with regard to our education."[9]

While in Easton, Margaret Junkin also began to compose stories and poems,
concentrating mostly on the latter.[10] According to a friend of hers at the time,
Junkin was at the center of a literary circle when she was just sixteen years old,
and her poetical talent was already known and admired.[11] In 1837 she began

copying her works into large notebooks. She took her hobby seriously and re-peatedly read over her writings, correcting and revising them. She found her inspiration in virtually everything she saw, heard, read, or experienced: family members, Bible stories, death, nature, and the classics. Junkin also wrote tributes to the early history of the United States, no doubt inspired by the tales of her grandfather's participation in the Revolution.[12] She discovered a special place in Easton where she could be alone to write and think, her own private retreat. It was a little nook amid a group of hawthorn trees on the bank of Bushkill Creek. She called it "Hawthorn Bower," and wrote a tribute with that title, explaining its significance in her life. The poem's concluding lines illustrate how important she felt it was to have a hideaway from the world:

> May no intruder enter here I claim this spot my own,
> Where I will often trust to find 'tis sweet to be *alone*
> Where I may come at early morn or at the twilight hour,
> And muse and dream my fancy dreams within my "Hawthorn Bower."[13]

As much as she enjoyed her writing, Junkin actually preferred another pas-time: painting.[14] While she was keeping her writing notebooks, she was also working in a sketchbook, drawing and watercoloring. Junkin usually depicted nature scenes, views of Bushkill Creek and other places in Easton.[15] Sometimes she painted flowers that baby sister Julia, born in June 1835, brought to her.[16] Junkin shared her passion with the eldest of her two sisters, Eleanor, and Eleanor contributed two paintings to the sketchbook: a bluebird and a cardinal.[17] The close relationship that the two sisters had shared as little girls continued as they became young women. In fact, when she was nineteen, Junkin wrote a poem to her beloved Eleanor, chronicling many of their activities together. In the final stanza of "Lines Addressed to Sister Eleanor," Junkin emphasized the strong bond between the two, a bond that she believed unbreakable, even in death:

> Together have we read
>   The poet's thrilling lays
> Together past have sped
>   Our childhood's sunny days
> Together may we be
>   For many a year to come
> Together may we be
>   In an eternal home![18]

Despite her many interests, Junkin found the time for a few, more typical teenage distractions. In Easton she fell in love for the first time, though she closely guarded the identity of the young man, never naming him in her note-books.[19] It appears that her love interest was not one of Lafayette's students, as might have been expected, but one of its faculty, Charles McCay. Junkin's friend and tutor had left Easton in 1834, when she was just fourteen years old, accepting a position at the University of Georgia.[20] But he visited Easton a couple of times after that, in 1838 and in 1839, and Eleanor believed it was for the purpose of courting her sister.[21] As close as the two sisters were, it is difficult to imagine that Junkin did not believe the same. Yet in 1840 McCay married a woman in Georgia. In reaction to the news, Junkin wrote him a long letter on November 13 of that year, entirely in rhyme. She told of her appreciation for the classical instruction he had given her, but her opening words indicate that her feelings for her mentor were deeper and more personal than those of a thankful pupil:

> I well remember all your care (would I had prized it more!),
> To open to my wayward mind the gems of Roman lore;
> When with you I o'ertraced the paths the pious Trojan roved,
> And sighed to think how fruitlessly the Tyrian Dido loved.
> And when I read the story now, beside me still you seem,
> And childhood's thoughts float o'er my heart, as mist floats o'er a stream.[22]

Junkin hinted that there had once been a romantic attachment between her and McCay, or at least that she had believed that to be the case: "Bride! thy lips have breathed the vow, / And thou art another's now."[23]

If Margaret Junkin was the "Tyrian Dido" who loved "fruitlessly," it remains a mystery as to why her love was ultimately unrequited. Perhaps McCay never saw more in Junkin than a student and friend, while Eleanor, and probably Junkin as well, had misread his intentions. On the other hand it is possible McCay's feelings for his student had grown as the precocious little girl evolved into an intelligent and talented young woman, and the two could not marry for other reasons.

Junkin wrote at least two poems about her lost love. Each one kept his identity a secret, but at least one was written almost immediately after the November letter.[24] In one of these works, written at the "Forks of the Delaware" and cryptically titled "To _____ _____," she expressed resentment that her intended appeared to be getting over her and intimated that he had found another love:

> Forget thee! yes—I will forget thee,
>   Tho' in the strife my heart should break;
> 'Twere better I had never met thee,
>   So much I've suffered for thy sake.
>
> . . . .
>
> And yet it *must* be—thou hast said it,
>   The struggle will be light for *thee;*

> The gloomy future—(how I dread it)
> Seems only desolate to *me*.
>
> Forget thee! yes, I will forget thee!
> However vain the boast may seem;
> I'll be as tho' I had not met thee,
> And all the past shall be a dream![25]

In anticipating a "gloomy future," Junkin was being a bit dramatic, but she was clearly an emotional young woman who was deeply hurt by her first love.

While Junkin was having her romantic troubles, her father was once again at odds with a board of trustees. This time the conflict was not about his religious beliefs but rather his disciplinary actions. The problem began early in 1840, when a student at Lafayette, Andrew Porter, intentionally cut another student on the knee. The faculty, with President Junkin's approval, suspended Porter until he acknowledged his guilt and submitted to a public reprimand. Porter, however, was a well-connected student. His father was David Rittenhouse Porter, then governor of Pennsylvania, and his uncle was James Madison Porter, president of the Lafayette College board of trustees.[26] A relatively minor incident therefore ballooned into a showdown with J. M. Porter and the trustees on one side and George Junkin and the faculty on the other. Each side argued that it held ultimate authority in student discipline. Students took sides, and some faculty members resigned. Even the congregation of the First Presbyterian Church was divided. Tensions mounted throughout the year until Dr. Junkin decided to end the matter the same way he had in Germantown: he found a new position. This time, though, the school was much farther from home. George Junkin agreed to become the new president of Miami University in Oxford, Ohio.[27]

It was Dr. Junkin's reputation as a strong disciplinarian that attracted Miami University's trustees. The university, founded in 1809, was going through a tumultuous period when its trustees decided in 1840 that a change in leadership was necessary. Though created by the U.S. Congress and established by the State of Ohio, Miami University was dominated by the Presbyterian Church. Most of its faculty were ordained Presbyterian ministers; many of its trustees were members of the church; and Robert Hamilton Bishop, its current president, was a Presbyterian. The faculty, trustees, and President Bishop were divided on several issues, including student discipline and whether to follow the Old School or New School within the Presbyterian Church. The selection of George Junkin was an abrupt departure from the mild disciplinary methods and liberal religious beliefs of President Bishop.[28] Such a drastic change was likely to cause further upset at the university, and Dr. Junkin's uncompromising nature did not help. Making matters even worse, President Bishop planned to remain on campus as a member of the faculty, thus providing his supporters with a constant reminder of his alleged mistreatment.[29] George Junkin's tenure as president of Miami University was destined to fail before he even arrived in Ohio.

Though he could not have been aware of how precarious his position at Miami already was, George Junkin had his own reasons to regret leaving Lafayette College. He had been the key figure in bringing the proposed school to life and had designed it according to his ideals. As he had at the Manual Labor Academy, he had even advanced his own funds to the college.[30] More than anyone else, his stake in Lafayette's success was deeply personal. In a letter to one of his supporters at the school, Dr. Traill Green, Dr. Junkin expressed bitterness at leaving Lafayette while trying to remain optimistic about his new position: "It is true that the wrath of the Porters hath driven me from Easton . . . but for the knowledge of this wrath and the Judge's [J. M. Porter's] plotting for the downfall of the College, my friends would not have presented my name to the Trustees of Miami University."[31] Even after he arrived in Ohio, George Junkin remained anxious about the situation at Lafayette, warning Green that the school would fail if Porter continued on as president of the board of trustees.[32]

In addition to his beloved Lafayette, Dr. Junkin also left behind many friends and supporters in Easton. Over the years there were certainly those individuals who had found themselves at the wrong end of George Junkin's strong will and intolerance; yet there were also those who appreciated what Dr. Samuel Gross called his "abundance" of "native kindness." When the Junkin family left Easton by boat for Philadelphia, on March 31, 1841, a spontaneous gathering lined the bank of the river. George Junkin led the group in prayer, praying for the town, its inhabitants, and for Lafayette. As the boat pulled away, according to a newspaper account at the time, a "most profound silence reigned . . . a strong evidence of the deep impression which the parting words of this good man made upon their hearts."[33]

Like her father's, Margaret Junkin's years in Ohio were not destined to be happy ones. This was the second time in fewer than ten years that she had left behind an environment in which she had found intellectual as well as personal happiness. Yet, unlike before, Junkin was not able to retreat into her studies after the move. Shortly after the Junkins arrived in Ohio, when Margaret Junkin was twenty-one, her eyes began to fail. She was forced to give up her studies for fear that she might lose her sight entirely, and she hardly read for the next seven years. It may have been Junkin's devotion to her studies that kept her from pursuing them, for she believed that her troubles were possibly caused by her habit of studying by candlelight. Junkin was devastated at this turn of events and took complete charge of the housekeeping in order to occupy herself. Many years later, when complimented on her scholarship, she retorted, "How can you speak of one as a scholar whose studies were cut short at twenty-one, never to be resumed!"[34]

Junkin did, however, continue to write, and it was perhaps because of the termination of her studies that she took her pastime to a new level. She began to publish her works, and, proud of her accomplishments, she kept scrapbooks chronicling her publishing career. Her stories and poems appeared in national magazines such as the *Southern Literary Messenger* and *Neal's Saturday Gazette* and in newspapers such as Philadelphia's *U.S. Gazette*.[35] Junkin was part of a growing trend in the early nineteenth century as more and more women published in such venues.[36]

Nevertheless, traditional expectations about women's place survived, and many thought it was unsuitable that a woman should appear in print. For that reason Junkin, like many women in the early stages of their careers, published anonymously.[37] Her works were either signed "M.J." or not signed at all. Frustrated with such an arrangement, Junkin added "M.J." in her own handwriting to those unsigned poems that she placed in her scrapbooks.

The first work Junkin published was a poem titled "The Early Lost."[38] Written on March 17, 1841, just days before she left Pennsylvania, it is a tribute to Sarah McElroy, a friend who had died earlier that year.[39] The poem provides comfort by describing Sarah's glorious life in heaven. This approach reflects Junkin's religious upbringing, and it was also a common way of dealing with death in the early nineteenth-century United States.[40] The opening lines of "The Early Lost" remind those who grieve the loss of Sarah that she is in a far, far better place:

> Fair spirit! thy home is a home of delight,
>> Unclouded by visions of care,
> Beside the still waters thou walkest in white,
>> In robes thou are worthy to wear.
> Thou knowest a joy that we cannot conceive,
>> In thy far away haven of rest,
> But bending in sorrow, we selfishly grieve,
>> And seem to forget thou art blest.[41]

Nevertheless in the next stanza Junkin did acknowledge that death brought an end to her friend's physical being and to the earthly pleasures that she had experienced:

> Yet ah! it is mournful to think thou hast passed
>> In the freshness of girlhood away,
> To think o'er thy beautiful form there is cast
>> A cold, heavy mantle of clay;
> To think when the gentle-voiced summer shall come,
>> To waken the flowers again,

> Thou still wilt sleep on in thy low, grassy home,
> And summer will call *thee* in vain![42]

The poem then delivered personal messages to each of Sarah's family members —her father, mother, sisters, and brothers—telling all of them that they would be comforted by her presence in heaven. Junkin concluded "The Early Lost" with the thought that all individuals can "calmly" go to their graves if they know their spirits are "blest."[43]

Regardless of its final lines, the second stanza of the poem is the most revealing of Junkin's true feelings. As a grown woman, she still felt some of the same fear and horror about death as when she was a six-year-old child seeing it for the first time. She was never able to look at a dead body as an adult, and, despite her efforts at concentrating on the glories of heaven, she could not help but be horrified by the physical finality of death, by a body being covered by a "cold, heavy mantle of clay."[44] The message of confidence in "The Early Lost" was one that Junkin herself was trying desperately hard to absorb.

Junkin's fear of death was more evident in another of her published works, "A Lament at the Bier of a Student." The poem was written while the Junkin family was living in Ohio and was inspired by the death of a member of Miami University's senior class.[45] Like "The Early Lost," "A Lament at the Bier of a Student" acknowledges death's physical finality but declares that the student's soul is "thrilling with joy" in heaven. Yet this time Junkin's struggle to concentrate on the afterlife is more apparent. She was issuing a command to herself as much as she was to any reader when she wrote:

> Turn from those moveless features—forget that cold, cold clay,
> And follow the freed spirit in its far flight away;
> Think of the dazzling visions that burst upon his view,
> And say if in his gladness we should not glory too![46]

Junkin expressed privately how haunted she was by the thought of death. In July 1841 she wrote a poem in one of her notebooks that she titled "When a Few Years Are Come, Then I Shall Go the Way Whence I Shall Not Return":

> I too shall die
> Like myriads who have trod the path of life
> Before me, I shall fold the mantle up
> In which I've walked this green and pleasant Earth
> And lay it in the chambers of the grave
>
> I've looked abroad upon this lovely world,
> And thought how beautiful a place 't would be

> If *Death* had never trod its verdure down
> But death is every where. . . . [47]

Visions of heaven, so prevalent in Junkin's published works and so commonly discussed in her society, did not provide her with real comfort.

Junkin's inability to conquer her fear of death with confidence in a glorious afterlife revealed that she was questioning her father's rigid Presbyterianism. She was developing into an individual with her own doubts, opinions, and interests. Though her father was the greatest influence on her early life, Junkin was also aware of the intellectual and cultural developments going on around her. As the Albert Barnes trial had demonstrated, the Calvinism of George Junkin was losing its influence over American society in the early nineteenth century, and romanticism—in many ways the logical opposite of Calvinism—was becoming a major vehicle of intellectual and cultural expression.[48] Characterized by a belief in the dignity and worth of the individual, romanticism was more in step with the nation's growing faith in democracy than was Calvinism. Romantics valued the emotional and imaginative over the rational. Nature was not as important for its own merits as it was for its impact on individuals.[49] Margaret Junkin was influenced by the romantic movement. In fact, one of her first published works was "The Fate of a Rain-Drop." Published in the *Southern Literary Messenger* in December 1842, the poem is about a raindrop—from "the breast of a beautiful cloud"—that lands inside a rose. There, it is discovered by a girl and her companion:

> 'Twas the joy of a moment. A beautiful girl
>   While straying through garden and bower,
> Paused lightly to show her companion the pearl,
>   That lay on the breast of the flower.
>
> "'Tis a chalice containing an exquisite draught,
>   Which Emily only shall sip,"
> He said as he gathered the rose-bud—she quaffed,
>   And the pearl was dissolved on her lip![50]

Junkin's raindrop represents the inductive reasoning used by the romantics. An element as small as a raindrop could represent nature and its effect on men and women.

In the United States romanticism was joined by another powerful force: nationalism. For this reason American romanticism was different from the romantic movements in Europe.[51] American writers searched for a national identity and a national purpose, at least partly to compensate for their country's lack of a past. By the early 1800s there was a general consensus that America's identity and mission rested on its revolution against Great Britain. The United States had already experienced a national revolution; therefore, it could lead others toward freedom and liberty and serve as an example that a nation based on these principles could survive and flourish.[52] Reflecting the spirit of the time, many works written by women concentrated on historical, political, and patriotic themes.[53] In "Song," a poem she published around 1842, Junkin portrayed the revolution against Great Britain as central to the definition of America and its purpose. She placed herself in revolutionary times and encouraged men to join the fight for freedom:

> Listen! Liberty is pleading
>   To be rescued from her foe!
> See, thy country's heart is bleeding,
>   Breaking 'neath oppression's blow,
>   Therefore, go!
>
> Spirit-heroes, too, are o'er us—
>   Pilgrim-martyrs spread again
> Their life's lesson all before us—
>   Shall its struggles and its pain
>   Plead in vain?
>
>   . . . .
>
> Then, by all their stern devotion,
>   By the countless woes they bore,
> Drive the despot o'er the ocean,
>   Back upon his island shore,
>   Evermore![54]

In mentioning the "Pilgrim-martyrs," Junkin reminded the reader that America was founded as the "foe" of "oppression." The Revolution was the continuation of the fight for liberty that the Pilgrims had begun a century and a half earlier. America's mission, thus, was to fight oppression. Great Britain, in Junkin's eyes, was the traditional oppressor. Her Anglophobia was at least partly the result of the family lore about her ancestors' persecution by the British on two separate continents.

Though Junkin's writing provided her with an intellectual outlet, the years in Ohio were difficult for her whole family. Her father's tenure at Miami University was, not surprisingly, tempestuous.[55] Dr. Junkin faced the usual opposition to his religious conservatism. In this case, since Miami was not technically a Presbyterian school, there were religious groups, mainly Methodists, who objected to his running the university in such a denominational fashion.[56] He also aroused the ire of the student body, which resented his firm disciplinarianism. One student even sent a false notice of Dr. Junkin's death to the *U.S. Gazette* in Philadelphia.[57] But it was George Junkin's position on slavery that provided the final blow to his presidency.[58]

Slavery had become such a source of conflict in national politics that in 1840 the infamous "gag rule" in Congress was made permanent. According to this policy, the House of Representatives automatically tabled any abolitionist petitions. Dr. Junkin had never directly confronted the slavery issue until he arrived in Ohio. In that state abolitionism had gained wide popularity by the early 1840s. This abolitionism was different from the abolitionism of the past. Previously antislavery movements in the United States had promoted relatively mild methods: gradual emancipation, compensation for slaveholders, and colonization, the resettlement of freed slaves outside the United States. But in the 1830s abolitionism became more militant. Activists argued that slavery was immoral and demanded immediate and unconditional freedom for slaves.[59] Slave owners were widely denounced. In Ohio the preacher Theodore Dwight Weld was largely responsible for stirring up opposition to slavery on moral grounds.[60] Having arrived in a climate of strong opinions based on moral assertions, a man of George Junkin's nature was going to develop an opinion of his own.

In September 1843 Dr. Junkin announced that opinion in an eight-hour speech given over two days before the Presbyterian Synod of Cincinnati. The title of the address clearly stated his position: *The Integrity of Our National Union, vs. Abolitionism: An Argument from the Bible, in Proof of the Position that Believing Masters Ought to be Honored and Obeyed by Their Own Servants, and Tolerated in, Not Excommunicated from, the Church of God.* George Junkin provided what he believed to be proof from both the Old and the New Testaments that slavery was tolerated in the Bible. Though slavery was mentioned in the Old Testament, he argued, God never prohibited it. In the New Testament, according to Dr. Junkin, the holding of slaves was also never expressly forbidden. In fact the New Testament recognized some masters as good men.[61] This argument was in step with the consensus reached by Southern Presbyterian theologians, who insisted that the Bible recognized slavery as a legitimate system. However, Dr. Junkin broke from their position when he concluded that this recognition did not mean slavery was not evil.[62] He explained that there was a difference between tolerating an act and sanctioning it: "I take the distinction before alluded to, that the Bible *tolerates* slavery. Now, *toleration* is *bearing with—enduring* a thing; and it implies, that the thing is viewed as an evil."[63]

In addition to his biblical interpretation, George Junkin also had a secular reason for wanting his fellow Northern Presbyterians to tolerate slavery. As the title of his speech indicated, he believed that abolitionism was a threat to the Union. If nonslaveholding states broke communion with slaveholding ones, he argued, a civil war would be the consequence: "Such a war as the world has never witnessed—a war of uncompromising extermination, that will lay waste this vast territory, and leave the despotic powers of Europe exulting over the fall of the Republic!"[64] By including this concern in a biblically based address, Dr. Junkin demonstrated the reverence he felt for the Union. As early as 1843, he was publicly expressing his fear that the country his father had fought to create might destroy itself over slavery.

Dr. Junkin proposed a solution to the slavery issue, one in keeping with the mild abolitionism of the past. He believed that the North should pity the South because it was "afflicted" with slavery and should help to emancipate the slaves through colonization. Yet he compared slaves to children and warned that they could not be set free immediately, only after they were "first educated and fitted to provide for themselves."[65] Such attitudes won George Junkin friends in unlikely places. In September 1846 Senator John C. Calhoun of South Carolina wrote to Dr. Junkin, stating: "I have read several able discussions on the same subject, but in none of them have the various passages of the Bible in reference to the subject of slavery been presented in so clear & systematick a manner, and discussed with such thorough knowledge of it, under all its aspects. You have left not a loop hole large enough for the most subtle & sophistical opponent to escape."[66]

Closer to home the abolitionists at Miami were less impressed. George Junkin had broken with the Southern argument that the Bible confirmed slavery was not an evil. However, his thoughts on toleration and colonization were unacceptable. After the speech the controversy surrounding the president was greater than ever.[67] Once again George Junkin extricated himself from an uncomfortable situation by accepting another position, this one from a surprising place. The Lafayette College board of trustees unanimously elected him president of their school on September 7, 1844.[68]

While George Junkin was struggling in Ohio, Lafayette had been having difficulties of its own. The new president was quarreling with the board, just as Dr. Junkin had, and faculty members were resigning. Meanwhile several events conjoined to increase the trustees' appreciation of Dr. Junkin: the enthusiasm for him shown at his departure, the false report of his death in the *U.S. Gazette,* and an address he gave at Lafayette in September 1842. That speech, given at the time of commencement, was titled "North America Is the Asylum and Home of Protestantism." It was so well received that, after Dr. Junkin had returned to Ohio, the college's literary societies requested a copy of it. He enclosed a letter with the speech, declaring "the fondest affections of this parent heart still cling" around

Lafayette. George Junkin accepted the board's offer on September 24, 1844, on the condition that he be given enough money to enable his family to live in town rather than on campus.[69]

The Junkins returned to Easton the next month.[70] As much as she had missed her old home, Margaret Junkin had not wanted her father to accept the position at Lafayette. She had evidently inherited her father's iron will, for she felt that he had been mistreated at the college and should not return regardless of how desirable it might be to do so. Nevertheless, once the Junkins arrived in Pennsylvania, she was happy to be back. She continued her writing and painting and enjoyed being surrounded once again by the beautiful Pennsylvania countryside.[71]

Yet Junkin was soon forced to abandon her painting permanently. Having already ceased her studies because of her failing eyesight, Junkin had a severe attack of rheumatic fever in 1845, which lasted for several months. Before she had sufficiently recovered, she became involved in the planning of a Christmas bazaar designed to help alleviate Lafayette College's debts. Junkin contributed a painting to the bazaar, an exertion that, according to her stepdaughter, caused the "first absolute breakdown with her eyes, and from which they never really recovered."[72]

Unable to paint, Junkin was still able to write, dictating her poems to Eleanor and her mother.[73] She continued to publish, submitting her dictated works, as well as works she had written in her notebooks years earlier.[74] One poem she composed during this time indicates that she had adopted some of the same views on slavery that her father had expressed while the family lived in Ohio. "A Ballad in Reply to Martin Farquhar Tupper's 'New Ballad to Columbia'" is Junkin's reaction to antislavery sentiment in England. She began the work by reminding the English of their own history of oppression, referring specifically to her ancestors, the Scots-Irish:

> We read of England's glories,
>   And own her proud control,
> We kindle o'er the record
>   Of Scotland's martyr soul;—
> We sigh o'er Erin's sorrows,
>   And wonder at the wrong,
> That should have bowed her children
>   So sadly and so long.[75]

She then argued that American slavery was the legacy of this tarnished history:

> Let Britain's sons remember
>   The old Colonial day,

> When o'er the sea-girt Islands,
>   The Maiden Queen held sway,
> *Whose* ships began the traffic,—
>   *Who* brought across the waves,
> Unwelcome to Virginia,
>   A human freight of slaves![76]

Like her father, Junkin believed that slavery was a "burden" for the United States. She longed for the day when the slaves, after being "christianised" and "enlightened" by their masters, could be sent to the land of their ancestors:

> Yes! hastened be the hour
>   When slavery—hateful word!
> Thro' all our pleasant borders,
>   Shall never more be heard;—
> When christianised—enlightened—
>   Out slaves shall walk abroad,
> Beneath their native sunshine,
>   The freemen of their God![77]

The poem was more than Junkin's declaration of her position on slavery, however. Its publication marked the first time that she allowed her full name to appear in print. In taking her career to this new level, Junkin became more vulnerable to charges that she was violating woman's prescribed role. Yet she also received nationwide recognition. In the late 1840s anthologies of American women poets were published for the first time, and Junkin's poems appear in several of them. In *The American Female Poets* (1848) Caroline May identified Junkin as the "daughter of the Rev. Dr. Junkin, a highly esteemed clergyman of the Presbyterian denomination, and the President of Lafayette College, Easton, Pennsylvania."[78] May included seventy-three poets in her anthology, arranging them chronologically with Junkin appearing next to last. May explained that women had little time to write because they were preoccupied with the "cares and duties of home" and that therefore the themes of female poets were usually from "every-day life." However, the poem of Junkin's that May included in *The American Female Poets* is "Galileo before the Inquisition."[79] Its subject matter demonstrates that, before her eyes began to fail, Junkin had received an extraordinary education while keeping up with her household duties.

The same year that *The American Female Poets* was published, in a pattern that had become all too familiar to Junkin, the family was once again uprooted after George Junkin had troubles with the Lafayette board of trustees. This time the problem began in October 1846, when Dr. Junkin tried to install his son

Joseph as principal of the academical department. The trustees rejected the appointment, and Dr. Junkin was furious. A quarrel ensued over whether the president or the board held the power of appointing professors. On September 19, 1848, Dr. Junkin delivered his resignation to a relieved board. He and his family were on their way to a very different world. George Junkin had accepted the presidency of Washington College in Lexington, Virginia.[80]

"An Intruder in the Field
of Literary Labor"

The Fight to Expand Woman's Place, 1848–1856

When Margaret Junkin left Pennsylvania near the end of 1848, she was already an unusual young woman. At the age of twenty-eight she had remained unmarried longer than most of her female friends or relatives. In the South she encountered even stronger expectations than she had in Pennsylvania that a woman her age should be married and raising a family. The average age at marriage of Southern women in Junkin's social class was nineteen, five years younger than the average age in the North. Furthermore Southern women had been slower than their Northern counterparts to press for changes in their civil standing; therefore they remained more constrained in the legal and public realms.[1] It is not surprising that women in the South had also been more hesitant in challenging the boundaries of the literary world.[2] In Virginia, Junkin's abilities and ambitions were destined to collide with woman's conscribed place.

There was much about Lexington, Virginia, that Junkin found appealing. Though it was a small town, about one-fourth the size of Easton, Lexington boasted a high degree of intellectualism and culture, owing not only to the presence of Washington College but also to that of the Virginia Military Institute. Most of the town's approximately one thousand white citizens were of Scots-Irish ancestry, like the Junkins. Lexington is located in the James River watershed immediately south of the Shenandoah Valley and is the seat of Rockbridge County. The county was named after the Natural Bridge, a rock formation fourteen miles south of Lexington that stands 93 feet high and 215 feet wide. Rockbridge County's population totaled 11,476 whites, 4,196 slaves, and 368 freedmen in 1850.[3] After having formulated strong opinions about slavery, Margaret Junkin and her father were living with the institution for the first time.

During her first few months in Virginia, Junkin was not concerned with finding her place in this new world. Rather she and the rest of the Junkin family were preoccupied with the condition of Joseph, the third Junkin child.[4] Joseph was suffering from pulmonary troubles, and George Junkin had assumed that Virginia's climate would keep his son's condition from worsening. Arriving in western Virginia during the winter, the Junkins quickly realized that Joseph should go further south.[5] John, the oldest Junkin boy, then a physician in Trenton, New Jersey, was called on to take his brother to Marianna, Florida. Throughout the winter, the family "lived upon letters from the South, now hopeful, now discouraging," as Margaret Junkin's stepdaughter later wrote. Hope for Joseph's recovery was abandoned by the spring of 1849, and his grief-stricken father wrote to John with the request that he bring his brother home to die. Yet, when George Junkin met the stagecoach as it arrived in Lexington, he was shocked to discover that only one of his sons was onboard. Joseph had died before he could be reunited with the rest of his family.[6]

The loss of her brother was a terrible blow to Margaret Junkin. Her old horror of death was intensified by having lost someone so close to her. She turned to her writing for solace and composed "The Hallowed Name," a poem in which she expressed her difficulty in speaking her late brother's name:

> I once could speak those simple words
> With gay and cheerful tone,
> And hear them fall from other lips
> As lightly as their own;
> But now my voice grows tremulous
> And low, as if it came
> Through sobs that choke me, when I breathe
> The old familiar name.[7]

The poem goes on—as do "The Early Lost" and "A Lament at the Bier of a Student"—to concentrate on the grave itself. The cold loneliness of the grave was amplified in Junkin's mind by her brother's having been laid to rest so far away from home:

> Far off, above a grave that lies
> Mid other graves unknown,
> Strange eyes now see it cut upon
> A monumental stone:
> They dream not, as the brief sad line
> They frame with thoughtless air,
> Through what a gush of tears my eyes
> Would read it graven there![8]

Yet in the conclusion, as in the previous works, Junkin provided comfort with the knowledge that Joseph was promised a glorious afterlife:

> Close hid within my brooding heart
> I keep that sacred word,
> Which midst the throngs of living men
> Shall never more be heard:
> *He* could not find on earth again
> Scope for his spirit's aim:
> Ah, since an *angel* bears it now,
> It *is* a hallowed name![9]

To her family Junkin admitted that such thoughts did not allay her suffering. In a letter to her brother George, written on May 4, 1849, a few weeks after Joseph's death, she commented on how their mother was handling the loss of her child: "Mother has been very much supported. She has not dwelt as much as I have upon the far-off, lonely grave, and the forsaken clay; but with a Christian's vision she follows the spirit of her darling child into the mansions which Jesus has prepared for those who love Him."[10] For the first time Junkin had openly hinted at a reason as to why she was so terribly haunted by death. She did not have the strong faith in the afterlife—the "Christian's vision," as she had termed it—of some members of her family. Hence she could not find comfort at the time of a death. Junkin told George she felt it would be "treason" to their brother's memory if they continued to find the same joy in life as they had previously. Later in her lifetime Junkin confessed to her loved ones that she believed the sorrow she felt at a death was "unchristian."[11]

Eventually, despite their loss, the Junkin family settled into a pleasurable existence in Lexington. The family lived on the campus of Washington College in the president's house. The college, originally founded in 1749 as a preparatory school for boys going into the Presbyterian ministry, was chartered as Liberty Hall Academy in 1782. It was later named in honor of George Washington. Though the college's charter was secular, the Presbyterian influence at the school was still pervasive. The president's house was a three-bedroom brick house that stood a few hundred yards from the classroom buildings. In addition to Margaret, three other siblings remained in the household: Eleanor, Julia, and William.[12] The family took long walks, venturing several miles from town and enjoying the picturesque scenery. Julia later recalled that the Junkins' adventures were surprising to the people of Lexington, "who were not quite so energetic."[13]

The residents of Lexington did, however, socialize frequently. "If we wished for some designation that would embrace a prevailing characteristic," Margaret Junkin wrote in a letter to Pennsylvania, "no better could be found than the '*visiting* Virginians'!" She went on to explain that "the ennui incident upon having to stay at home for a few days, without having company or being company, is considered quite insupportable."[14] According to Julia, her oldest sister very much enjoyed the "delightful" conversations she had at social functions with the "many cultivated men" connected with the schools. Mrs. Junkin, now severely hard of hearing, went out little, and her daughters always sat with her after their return and told her everything, "so that she did not feel so cut off from the world around her as many deaf people do."[15] The young women also attended more informal gatherings. Margaret Junkin described a typical all-female gathering in an 1852 letter: "A circle of us were sitting around the wide parlor hearth one morning; the young ladies busy with their crocheting and needle-work of various kinds, and I reading aloud to them [Nathaniel] Hawthorne's new book, 'The Blithedale Romance,' which I had slipped into the pocket of the carriage to beguile the way with, in case E. [Eleanor] might not be in a talkative mood."[16]

By bringing her literary interests to the group of young women, Junkin was attempting to create a place for herself in Lexington society, one that brought her masculine interests into the feminine world. She could have chosen an easier course and curtailed her literary activities, which in turn might have attracted an otherwise intimidated suitor. But with her father's strong will she remained on the more difficult path. Her writing had become a source of pride, an outlet for her intellectual energies, and a part of who she was. From February 1849 to June 1854, Junkin published poems, stories, and translations in such prestigious journals as *Graham's American Monthly Magazine of Literature and Art* and *Sartain's Union Magazine of Literature and Art.* She was a frequent contributor to the *Southern Literary Messenger,* appearing in its pages eighteen times between February 1849 and February 1853.

Junkin not only continued her writing, but she also used it in a quest to gain acceptance for herself and for other female authors. In the *Sartain's* of January 1852, she published a short story, "The Reconcilement of the Real and the Ideal," in which she argued that women could successfully perform both traditionally male and traditionally female activities. The "real" represents what was considered woman's work—cooking, sewing, cleaning; while the "ideal" represents the male domains of writing, art, and scholarship. The story unfolds as a friendly argument between two friends, Woodward and Cleaveland. Woodward, the elder of the two men, is an artist who believes that women can be authors and still successfully fulfill their domestic duties. Cleaveland, a student, feels that women encroach on the "prerogatives of the other sex, when they assume the pen." However, he believes that, if a woman is truly talented, then she should devote herself to literary endeavors and nothing else. A woman interested in literary distinction, according to Cleaveland, will necessarily grow weary of "the homeliness, the commonplace, of domestic life" and should be "completely set apart." Woodward counters with the argument that such a woman's "sense of the beautiful would manifest itself in her household arrangements." Unable to convince his friend, Woodward decides to provide him with a living example.[17]

The character of Dora Vincent displays many similarities to Margaret Junkin. She is the eldest daughter of a highly educated man, who has in turn educated his daughters. Dora writes poetry, "real, 'solemn-thoughted idyls,'" reads classical languages, and takes drawing lessons from Woodward. She also prepares jellies and bakes muffins that lift Cleaveland "into the regions of nectar and ambrosia."[18] Several times Junkin clearly juxtaposed Dora's two worlds. As Cleaveland admires her extensive collection of great literary works, he sees a thimble and spools of cotton nearby. Later Cleaveland discovers Dora's younger sister, Annie, busy putting her sibling's books away. Just after Annie explains that Dora wakes up early every morning to study, Dora appears in the doorway, hands full of fresh flowers. Of course Cleaveland is convinced that "the real and the ideal" can be reconciled, and he and Dora fall in love.

"The Reconcilement of the Real and the Ideal" represents Junkin's hope for her own life, that she would be accepted as a publishing author. Yet the argument she used, that she and other women like her would not necessarily neglect their domestic duties, reinforced the traditional restraints placed on women. Junkin's heroine has to master both the male and female domains, while Cleaveland has only to master the male's to be worthy of Dora's hand. That Dora's ultimate happiness is achieved through a relationship with a man also demonstrates that Junkin was bowing to conventional standards and hints at her own hopes of finding a man who would accept her. She might not have been willing to give up her writing, but she also was not challenging the domestic ideal.

In addition to this new subject matter, Junkin explored more familiar themes during this period as well. Her published religious works still tried to conceal doubts and fears. One short story, "Julia: A Sketch of Ancient Rome," which appeared in *Sartain's* in July 1851, celebrates the courage and convictions of persecuted Christians in ancient Rome even when faced with such horrors as being "torn to pieces by dogs."[19] "Julia" also displays Junkin's impressive knowledge of history, as do two works in the *Southern Literary Messenger,* a ballad about the death of William the Conqueror and a story based on the final days of England's King Henry II.[20] Her knowledge of foreign languages is demonstrated by translations from both French and Greek texts.[21]

Junkin continued in the romantic tradition, particularly in the poem "An Apostrophe to Niagara," which appeared in the *Southern Literary Messenger* of August 1849.[22] During the first half of the nineteenth century, Niagara Falls was the best-known icon of nature in the United States. In fact the falls had become a symbol of America. Niagara Falls and George Washington were the most often painted subjects in the country's art. Junkin had never visited the falls, but literary descriptions and pictures were widely disseminated. Poetry about Niagara

Falls was common, and "An Apostrophe to Niagara" shares traits with many of these works. Junkin's poem reflects the romantic interest in the effects of nature on individuals. She used several of the words employed by other authors to describe the experience of seeing the falls, words such as *wonder, stupendous,* and *abyss.* The term *sublime* was the ultimate expression of powerful reaction to the falls.[23] Junkin employed this word twice:

> The gazer's soul with such sublimity,
> That thought withdraws dismayed, serenely stands,
> A *silent* witness of its Builder's power;
> Whilst thou, sublimer still, doth make appeal
> To the amazed and awe-struck ear no less
> Than to th' enraptur'd, overflowing eye![24]

Much Niagara poetry refers to the double nature of this sublime experience, pointing out that the falls are as terrifying as they are beautiful.[25] Junkin's work is no exception:

> I tremble as I gaze:—and yet my soul
> Revives again with this indwelling thought;—
> That though thy stunning torrent pour itself
> In undiminished volume, on and on,
> For centuries unsumm'd,—there *is* a time,
> When all that makes thee now so terrible,
> (Yet in thy greatest terror, lovely still,)
> Shall sink to silence quiet as the grave.[26]

Junkin also continued to express the country's nationalistic impulses. In 1848 nationalism reached a fever pitch in the United States as a result of the revolutions sweeping through Europe. Revolution began in France and quickly spread to Germany, Italy, and the Hapsburg Empire, with the rebels demanding constitutional governments. Here was what American nationalists had anticipated: the United States had served as an example of revolution in favor of freedom and liberty. Events in Hungary especially captured American interest. In the last of the series of European revolutions, Louis Kossuth led the Magyars in a rebellion against the Hapsburgs. Though Kossuth's struggle was a complicated blend of antimonarchical sentiment and ethnic rivalry, the American people saw him as a crusader for liberty and republicanism.[27]

Margaret Junkin's corner of the country participated in the near obsession with Kossuth's campaign. In Richmond, Virginia, Robert Tyler, son of a former president of the United States, announced that he would raise troops to join in the fighting. But the struggle was over quickly. The revolutionaries were no match for the combined force of the Austrian army and the Hapsburg ally

Russia. Kossuth fled to Turkey in August 1849, and the Hungarians officially surrendered days later. Hungary was back under monarchical rule; Kossuth was
jailed in Turkey, possibly facing extradition; and his family was in exile.[28]

In Kossuth's tale Junkin found the inspiration for the poem that represents
the culmination of her nationalistic thought. While in Turkey, Kossuth wrote to
Henry John Temple, Lord Palmerston, British foreign secretary, to tell him of his
family's homeless condition. Junkin's poem "Kossuth," published in the May
1850 issue of *Sartain's,* declares that Kossuth and his family could make their
home in the United States. After opening her poem with jabs at those nations
that had not come to Hungary's aid—England and France—as well as a con-
demnation of the country that had helped crush the rebellion—Russia—she
concluded with an invitation:

> Come with thy precious household band,
>   And share the gifts by Fate denied
> Thine own beloved and stricken land,—
>   Gifts, which to win, our fathers died.
> Come then, and share the heritage
>   Bequeathed by them to all opprest,
> Of every race, and every age:—
>   Where find so fit a place of rest,
> For Freedom's homeless, banished son,
> As in the land of Washington![29]

Junkin had taken the message she had conveyed in her 1842 poem "Song" to its
logical conclusion. America was founded as the foe of oppression; it would serve
as the sanctuary for all who were oppressed.

While Junkin remained proud of her native country, she was growing fond
of her adopted state. In April 1849 she published a tribute to Virginia, "The Old
Dominion: A Ballad," in the *Southern Literary Messenger.* This work celebrates
Virginia's history as the first permanent English settlement, her participation in
the American Revolution, and, in particular, the famous men who had called the
state their home:

> Virginia! brave Virginia!—a happy Mother thou,
> Whose children's fame will ever shed a splendor round thy brow;
> The thrilling words of eloquence that Henry's fervor flung;
> The simple majesty of thought that flowed from Marshall's tongue,—
> The force and skill political which Jefferson could show,
> The statesmanship of Madison,—the wisdom of Munroe [sic].[30]

Yet by poem's end, despite all of Virginia's fine qualities, Junkin remained most
loyal to her home state of Pennsylvania:

But now from all these glowing scenes my thoughts return again,
With filial reverence to thee, dear sylvan land of Penn!
Thou, too, canst boast a thousand charms that make thy vallies bright,—
O'er which affection sweetly pours a flood of golden light;
Thy shaded homes lie lovingly by many a sparkling stream,
Thy rivers, mountains, fields and groves,—how beautiful they seem!

Beside Virginia's would I place thy justly honored name,
And claim equality for thee upon the scroll of fame;
But while with admiration deep, I humbly dedicate,
A heart of zealous loyalty to my adopted state,—
Yet true to all my earliest love, I still will turn again
With fondlier feelings far to you, oh! sylvan shades of Penn.[31]

As Junkin continued to live in Virginia, her attitude about slavery began to change. Before moving to the South, she had come to agree with her father that the region should be pitied for being burdened with the institution and that the best solution for both slaveholders and slaves alike was colonization. Once they arrived in Lexington, the Junkins found attitudes similar to their own. Since the slave rebellion led by Nat Turner in 1831, there had been strong support in Virginia for colonization. In 1833 the state legislature pledged to spend eighteen thousand dollars per year for five years on colonizing efforts. By 1850 that number had increased to thirty thousand dollars per year, also for a period of five years.[32] In December 1849 a rally was held in Lexington to commemorate the departure of a group of immigrants to Liberia. Junkin wrote a poem for the gathering, and Reverend Junkin was involved in the planning as well. In "Stanzas" Junkin expressed her belief that slavery had christianized and enlightened the now freedmen. Yet she did acknowledge some of the ugly aspects of slavery and stated that, when they arrived "home," the former slaves would no longer be oppressed:

> *Home,* where the hopes now center,
>   That once were vague and vain—
> Where bondage cannot enter,
>   To bind them down again:—
> *Home*—free from all oppressions,
>   *Home*—where the palm-tree waves,
> *Home*—to their own possessions—
>   *Home*—to their grandsires' graves![33]

But Junkin soon dropped any references to the evils of slavery. Though Rockbridge County was not as dependent on slave labor as many counties in Virginia, slaves still composed about one-fourth of the population. As time wore on, the Junkins grew more comfortable with slavery, and George Junkin became a slave-holder himself.[34]

Margaret Junkin quickly joined the growing chorus of those who argued that slavery was a positive experience for master and slave alike. The South was becoming increasingly defensive of the institution; Southerners were moving away from the almost apologetic argument that slavery was a "necessary evil" and toward unabashedly supporting it as a "positive good." The 1852 publication of Harriet Beecher Stowe's *Uncle Tom's Cabin,* in particular, inspired an outpouring of literature in defense of slavery.[35] Several of the Southern women who had entered the literary world by this time used their writing to attack Stowe, Caroline Hentz and Louisa McCord among them. Margaret Junkin did the same in a series of articles for Easton newspapers, written in the form of letters to a fictional friend. In her "letter" of September 9, 1852, while musing about what she and the "friend" might do if the latter came to Virginia for a visit, Junkin speculated that they might argue about *Uncle Tom's Cabin:* "I . . . would grow half angry at the one-sided book, and we should well-nigh quarrel about the mooted subject, when the sight of *Homer's* happy, care-free, black face and sleek, well-conditioned person, set becomingly off in white pants and apron, as he comes to announce dinner, should clinch *my* argument, and bring you over to a more correct way of thinking, before you had got through with your soup."[36]

Later, in a "letter" dated November 25, 1852, Junkin told the story of a slave wedding.[37] The story emphasizes several of the themes prevalent in proslavery literature at the time: the kindness of the slaveholder toward his slave, the attachment of the slave to his owner, and the carefree life of the slave.[38] In Junkin's tale she tells how she and Eleanor were visiting at the house of their friends the "G." family on the day that one of the "G." slaves, Rhinie, was to be married. "Mrs. G." had allowed the slaves to use the summer dining room for the festivities and had loaned them her table linens and china. The "G.'s" younger daughters were excitedly helping with the preparations, finding Rhinie a veil to wear and weaving wreaths for the cakes, since Rhinie was "scarcely less" important to them than "one of their sisters." Rhinie, for her part, admired and imitated the girls in the "G." family and wanted to look as much as possible like "Miss Maria," an older "G." daughter, "who had been the object of her most unbounded admiration when she had been married the year before." The two Junkin sisters attended the wedding ceremony, after which they and their friends returned to the parlor. Margaret Junkin described the ensuing merriment: "I wish, J., you could have heard the merry *haw-haws* that reached us in the parlor, as we sat with our coffee-cups in our hands round the well-filled waiter which had been despatched to us. If you had, I do not think your heart would have been disposed to waste much superfluous commiseration upon the so-called 'poor unhappy slaves.' After the supper was fully over, you should have heard the tum-tum-ing of the banjo, and the echo of the noisy feet that kept time to it."[39]

The cozy picture Junkin painted is belied by several offhand remarks that indicate just how far beneath the "white ladies" the slaves actually were. As the young ladies entered the dining room, according to Junkin, "the smiling and tittering and grinning groups rose to acknowledge the favor done them." At the close of her story Junkin stated: "Your inference may be that Rhinie would be quite spoiled by all this fuss about her. Not at all, my dear. The next morning we found her at our bedside, very little after the usual hour, dressed in her neat, everyday, linsey 'coat' . . . , quite ready to do our bidding."[40] Junkin might have been challenging the place that she, as a white woman, occupied in Southern society, but she accepted that she maintained a position above the black slave.[41]

Junkin had made a comfortable life for herself in Lexington, even though her writing career and unmarried status made her unusual. She enjoyed her contacts with the men at the colleges, and had developed friendships with several women as well. The most important part of her social life was her relationship with her sister Eleanor. The two women were inseparable and did almost everything together: horseback riding, domestic chores, even socializing. But in the fall of 1852 things began to change. Eleanor was being courted by a young professor at the Virginia Military Institute, Thomas Jonathan Jackson. Jackson had joined that school's faculty in August 1851. Twenty-seven years old at the time of his appointment, Major Jackson could already look back on a distinguished career. He had graduated from West Point in 1846, seventeenth in a class of fifty-nine. Immediately after graduation, he joined the fighting in the Mexican War and was commended for his actions in that conflict. Standing at five feet eleven inches, Jackson was a tall man, with brown hair and a ruddy complexion. His side whiskers extended from his ears down to his jaws, stopping short of his chin. He had a high forehead and dark blue eyes. Jackson's stern and humorless demeanor, coupled with his monotonous lectures, made him an obvious target for jokes. His students, for instance, often drew a figure with huge feet on his blackboard, poking fun at one of his more prominent physical characteristics.[42] Margaret Junkin, aware of Jackson's reputation, did not think that the major was suitable for her sister. Eleanor, no doubt seeing in Jackson what the community —and, indeed, the world—later saw, fell in love with him, and by early 1853 the two were engaged.[43]

The news was devastating to Junkin. Her reasons no doubt went far deeper than her personal feelings about Jackson, for she was losing her life's closest companion. In addition the fact that her younger sister was to be married at age twenty-eight surely underscored her own still-unmarried status. She would be more of an outsider than ever. Years later Junkin wrote that at this time she believed she would never marry. Junkin was so upset at this turn of events that

Eleanor, displaying a touching devotion to her older sister, called off the engagement.[44]

But Junkin loved her sister too much to stand in the way of her happiness. She again turned to her writing for solace and for a way to express her feelings. Echoing the poem she had written to Eleanor years earlier, "To My Sister" recounts how close the sisters had been in childhood. But it goes on to tell how that closeness has rightfully given way to Eleanor's relationship with Jackson:

> From very childhood's years, darling,
> We've known no separate joy;
> Whatever grieved *your* spirit, brought
> To mine the same annoy.
> Together, o'er one page we bent;
> Our kindred hearts have strayed
> Together through life's summer walks,
> In sunshine and in shade.
>
> But now our paths diverge, darling—
> A thought I cannot share
> Has seized your heart's high sovereignty,
> And rules supremely there.
> Yet while, as if discrowned of love,
> I feel an exile's pain,
> Believe me, that I question not
> That sovereign's right to reign.[45]

Though the poem is Junkin's way of telling her sister that she supported her marriage, it nevertheless makes clear the pain that she still felt:

> Forgive these sadden'd strains, darling—
> Forgive these eyes so dim;
> I must—*must* love whom *you* have loved—
> So I will turn to him;
> And clasping with a seeming clasp,
> Whose tenderness endears,
> Your hand and his between my own,
> I bless you through my tears.[46]

Soon after her sister's poetic gesture, Eleanor resumed her engagement. The couple was married on August 4, 1853, in the parlor of the Junkin home with George Junkin officiating.[47]

It was only after Jackson had won the hand of Eleanor Junkin that he began to win the admiration, respect, and even love of the rest of the Junkin family, Margaret included. One of the first things the Junkins learned about Jackson was that he was an extremely modest man. The family did not even hear of his distinguished record of service in the army during the Mexican War until after he had asked Eleanor to marry him. Shortly after the wedding, Margaret Junkin learned of what she later called Jackson's "military enthusiasm." She had accompanied the newlyweds on a wedding trip to Canada and Niagara Falls. In Quebec on the Plains of Abraham, the site of the 1759 victory of the British over the French, the threesome visited the monument erected to General James Wolfe. As he approached the monument, Jackson took off his cap. "He turned his face towards the setting sun," Junkin later wrote, "swept his arm with a passionate movement around the plain, and exclaimed, . . . 'To die as *he* died, who would not die content!'"[48]

On their return to Lexington the newlyweds moved into the Junkin home. The household consisted of Reverend and Mrs. Junkin, thirty-three-year-old Margaret, eighteen-year-old Julia, and the Jacksons. Margaret Junkin's physical proximity to Eleanor did not allay her feeling that her sister was forever lost to her. She grew increasingly lonely and anticipated spending the remainder of her days unmarried and childless. For her part Eleanor was evidently too happy to be affected by her sister's state of mind.[49]

Yet a monumental event was about to occur in the sisters' lives, one that would jar Eleanor's newfound happiness and catapult Junkin further into grief. After a protracted illness, their mother, Julia Miller Junkin, died on February 23, 1854. Eleanor, possessed of a strong faith, weathered the ordeal relatively well. But Margaret, in her usual fashion, descended into a spiral of doubt, fear, and depression.[50] Displaying a tendency she had first exhibited as a little girl, Junkin completely withdrew from those around her, a tactic that served only to compound her grief. She already felt that Eleanor was lost to her as an emotional support, and she never considered turning to her father or sister Julia.[51] In the poem Junkin wrote after her mother's death, "Left Behind," it is clear that her isolation was both real and self-imposed:

> What matters it that other eyes
> > Have smiles to give me just as sweet,
> > Or softly other lips repeat
> Endearments of as gentle guise?
> I only feel the smile, whate'er
> > Its yearning tenderness may be,
> Is not the one whose winning cheer
> > Was more than all the world to me!
> I only feel, howe'er so kind
> > Is everything that voice may say—
> 'Tis not the one that passed away,
> > When I was left behind![52]

Throughout her lifetime, since she was a child of six, the death of someone she knew had sent Junkin into a tailspin of emotions, more so if she had been close to the deceased. She did not turn to others for support, but, when she was older, she at least had her writing as a source of comfort. There was one death, however, that Junkin did not know how to deal with, even in her writing. On October 22, 1854, just eight months after the death of Mrs. Junkin, Eleanor died after giving birth to a stillborn son. Eleanor's death was the last in a series of traumatic events that had begun a little more than a year before, and Margaret Junkin's health—no doubt affected by her emotions—was failing. Soon after Eleanor's death, she traveled to Philadelphia to stay with her brother George. Jackson remained in the Junkin home with George Junkin and Julia.[53]

In an effort to cope with the loss of her sister, Junkin turned to a surprising source of comfort: her brother-in-law, Major Jackson. On December 19, Jackson received a letter from Junkin. "My dear Brother," she began, "I feel an irresistible desire to write you today—for my heart has been so exceedingly oppressed in dwelling upon our loss, that perhaps to write to you may be some relief. It may seem selfish to go to you to pour out some of my sorrow—you have more than enough of your own to bear." Junkin asked Jackson to reply to her but stated that she would "know why [if] you don't." She requested that he at least pray for her and think of her "always, [as] your most affectionate and sympathizing sister."[54]

Jackson did reply, on February 14, 1855. He apologized for not having written sooner, telling Junkin that she would "well know the reason why" he had not done so. He then went on to explain why he was willing to establish a loving relationship with Junkin, despite her past feelings: "You and I were certainly the dearest objects which she [Eleanor] left on earth. And if her emancipated Spirit comes back to earth, and sees how we are bound together, and how we have a mutual bond of strong affection for *her,* do you not suppose that it thrills her with delight?"[55] Jackson did admonish Junkin a bit, suggesting that "such [Eleanor's delight at their 'mutual bond of strong affection'] would have been the case when [she was] here."[56] Jackson continued, demonstrating that he now felt very much a part of the Junkin family: "When I stood by her [Eleanor's] grave, and that of Mother [Julia Junkin] last Saturday, they were both covered with snow; though their bodies rested beneath the cold covering, yet was it not in color emblematic of their spiritual robes of white?"[57] The remainder of Jackson's letter made it clear that the major was possessed of a strong faith, the kind of faith that Junkin yearned for, that helped carry him through his terrible grief.[58]

This letter began an exchange of correspondence between Junkin and Jackson that resulted, in Jackson's words, in their drawing "nearer to each other."[59] After Junkin returned home in April, she began a habit of visiting Jackson in his study nearly every night at nine o'clock. There, the two would talk for an hour or two. "In such intercourse," Junkin later wrote, "I came to know the man as never before. His early life, his lonely orphanage, his struggle with disease, his West Point life, his campaigning in Mexico, . . . his life at various posts up to the time of his coming to reside among us,—all these furnished material for endless reminiscence." Junkin learned that the stern military man had a "sportive, rollicking side." At times, he would be so amused during their conversations that he would nearly "roll from his chair in laughter."[60]

Junkin also learned that many of Jackson's idiosyncrasies were the result of what she later called "the deepest underlying principle." For example, one evening Junkin overheard a conversation between Jackson and a friend. At one point, according to Junkin, the friend said, "You remember, Major, that at this period Lord Burleigh was Queen Elizabeth's great counselor." Interrupting the man, Jackson exclaimed, "No, I don't remember, for I did not know it." Afterward Junkin teased the major for his lack of charm with their friend. Jackson explained that to him absolute truth was of far greater importance than conversational grace.[61]

Junkin's relationship with Jackson might have somewhat assuaged her loneliness, but at thirty-five years old she still had no prospects of marriage and family and remained squarely outside the norm.[62] She poured her feelings of isolation into a short story, "The Child of Song," which received a fifty dollar prize from the *Dollar Newspaper* of Philadelphia. She chose to sign the work "M.J." rather than to divulge her full name, perhaps because of her increasing awareness of the social cost of her notoriety. "The Child of Song" is largely autobiographical, and this too may have affected Junkin's decision to remain anonymous. The tale is about a twenty-two-year-old woman named Adalaide who, her age notwithstanding, has many things in common with Junkin. Adalaide, who is a Southerner, is scared to love because she has experienced so much loss. Her sister died about a year before the story takes place and her mother before that. Adalaide writes poetry to help deal with her pain and has already published some of her works. Yet she has found that it is not acceptable to be both a woman and an author: "But what business has a *woman* with authorship? Is she not looked upon as an intruder in the field of literary labor? Is she not constantly reminded that *home* is her province, and that her utmost ambition should extend no farther than to dress the garden of *man's* heart and plant affections there? She must content herself with this sphere, nor ever venture out, Ruth-like, to glean behind the reapers."[63]

Whereas "The Reconcilement of the Real and the Ideal" is about hope—the hope that Dora Vincent (and, by extension, Margaret Junkin) can continue her writing and find a man who accepts her for what she is—"The Child of Song" is about despair. Such a man is not going to come along, so Adalaide asks if she could be accepted as an author if her home were bare: "Yet what if 'the flowers and fruits of love are gone,' and the garden is a waste, may she [a woman] not then wander forth and seek a grain of nourishment in the broad field?"[64] Despite her loneliness Junkin did not allow Adalaide, or herself, to give up her writing. Nevertheless Adalaide's heartbreak continues to the end of the tale, when she dies on hearing of another loved one's death.

During this period Junkin also wrote cheerier, less personal short stories. The subject matter of "The Virginia Colonist; A Story of Early Times," exhibits Junkin's growing identification with her adopted state and its history. "The Ashburnes; A Tale of Seventy-Seven," won a fifty dollar prize from the *Dollar Newspaper* of Philadelphia, just as "The Child of Song" had. Its subject matter harkens back to the stories of the Revolution, and her grandfather's participation in it, she had heard as a child.[65]

Junkin's concentration on short stories led her to write her first and only novel. By the 1850s novels by and about women had become extremely popular in the United States. In fact it was in 1855—frustrated that books by many women novelists were outselling his—that Nathaniel Hawthorne wrote his famous comment about the "mob of scribbling women."[66] Most of these women's works constituted a genre known as domestic fiction. They told tales of heroines facing dire circumstances; they met their trials with virtue and were rewarded with marriage. Southern domestic novelists differed from their Northern counterparts, for their works also incorporated a defense of their region.[67] Many women in the South, including Caroline Gilman and Caroline Hentz, were either supporting their families or supplementing their families' incomes with their royalties.[68] Junkin decided that she was as talented as many others and that she should "coin her brain into dollars," as she later wrote.[69]

The result, *Silverwood: Book of Memories,* was published anonymously in 1856, despite the publisher's offer to pay Junkin an additional sum if she would allow the use of her name.[70] Again, as with "The Child of Song," Junkin's refusal to sign her name may have been partly owing to the novel's autobiographical content. According to Junkin, she wrote *Silverwood* to "embalm the characters of dear mother, Ellie, and brother Joe."[71] The book is about a family named Irvine. There are four daughters—Edith, Zilpha, Eunice, and Josepha—and one son, Lawrence. The patriarch of the Irvine family has died before the story begins.[72] Mrs. Irvine, whom Junkin patterned after her mother, possesses brown hair, hazel eyes, and an "unusual youthfulness of complexion." She is not beautiful "in the common acceptation of the term," but her kind, caring nature makes her appear that way. Lawrence, who represents Junkin's deceased brother Joseph, is similar to his mother, only more reserved. He has wavy, auburn hair and a fair complexion. There is a "winning dignity" about his appearance, and he is thoroughly devoted to his mother.[73]

Junkin's description of Eleanor, through the character of Zilpha, is not as detailed. Zilpha's personality is revealed mainly by comparison with that of Edith, her eldest sister, who is obviously modeled on the author herself. Whereas Zilpha's spirit is "self-contained, equable," Edith's is "passionate, impulsive." Zilpha and her mother share a strong faith, which allows them to face every tragedy with a "calm state of acquiescence." Edith, on the other hand, worries that she "look[s] backward and forward too much, and *upward* too little." While both Mrs. Irvine and Lawrence die in *Silverwood,* it is interesting that Zilpha does not; she leaves the story by getting married.[74]

To Edith, Zilpha's marriage is nothing short of tragic. Edith likens the event to a death, stating that "the grave of marriage [is now] dug between us."[75] Here Junkin was drawing on her feelings regarding the union of Eleanor and Major Jackson. Perhaps Zilpha does not die in *Silverwood,* like Lawrence and Mrs. Irvine, because Junkin truly believed that Eleanor was lost to her before her actual death. Or perhaps the loss of her sister through marriage was the only loss that Junkin had the strength to face. Junkin had referred to Eleanor's death in her writing once in the previous two years and then only by mentioning that Adalaide's younger sister died before "The Child of Song" began.

Whatever her reasons for keeping Zilpha alive, Junkin gave that character's marriage equal weight to the many calamities that occur within the pages of *Silverwood.* The Irvine family loses half its money when a bank goes out of business. Later the Irvine home burns down, and a dishonest man absconds with the remaining family funds. There are also, of course, the deaths of Lawrence and Mrs. Irvine. But in keeping with the domestic novel format, Edith endures all this tragedy and is rewarded with a husband at story's end.

In "The Child of Song" Junkin—despite her loneliness—had still argued for women to be accepted as publishing authors. But in *Silverwood* she made no such attempt. Asked if she agrees with the "Amazonian tribe" who were fighting for women to enjoy a "wider sphere," Edith responds: "By no means! I'm perfectly content to have the barriers just where they are, since I believe Providence designed this circumscription. I firmly believe our sex was commanded to be 'under obedience,' as part of the primal curse."[76] But Edith makes it clear that she hopes for the day when this arrangement is changed: "Our [woman's] regeneration is being worked out as Christianity makes progress; and who knows but that the balances may be even, by the time we have reached the edge of the millenium [*sic*]."[77] Resigned to the fact that notions of woman's place were not going to change in her lifetime, Edith does what is expected of her: by novel's end she has found a husband. This development is so meaningful to Edith that it infuses her with the strong faith of her mother and sister.

She might have surrendered in her battle to expand woman's place, but Junkin made no secret of her frustration with that place. At one point Edith tells a gathering of friends that genius is a curse for women because "genius demands a wide range—an unobstructed field for its exercise—and that is not allotted us; or, if so, granted stintedly and grudgingly." She comments on the price paid by women who publish their writings, stating that they take the "public into partnership—so *it* thinks; and a thousand things, thenceforth, wound her [their] sensitive womanhood." In sharp contrast with Dora, the heroine of "The Reconcilement of the Real and the Ideal," who is just as happy baking muffins as she is composing poetry, Edith complains that "woman's duties" grow "irksome" to intellectual women. Expecting such women to perform these duties, she says, is like "setting a steam-engine to boil a tea-kettle."[78] In the fewer than ten years since she had written "The Reconcilement of the Real and the Ideal," Junkin had realized that her approach in that piece—to argue that women would not neglect their domestic duties if they were allowed a wider scope—was not going to work. She had also abandoned the argument of "The Child of Song"—that women without a domestic life should be welcomed into the man's domain. In *Silverwood*, therefore, Junkin was both traditional and progressive. She stopped fighting for women to be accepted outside of the home; yet she refuted her previous assertion that all women enjoyed, and should perform, their duties within the home.[79]

Junkin's attitude about slavery had remained far more consistent since she had moved to Lexington. In fact *Silverwood* manages to extol the merits of Liberia while also depicting happy, carefree slaves and loving masters. Slavery is shown as an open institution rather than as one characterized by bondage; the slaves in the novel are given a choice between staying on the plantation or moving to Liberia. Those who choose to leave write letters to their loved ones expressing satisfaction with their new lives, while those who stay are perfectly content, attached to their homes and their masters. Though Junkin's criticisms of domesticity are unusual, her defense of slavery is similar to that in other Southern domestic novels.[80]

Silverwood was not the financial success that Junkin had hoped it would be, and its publication did not significantly alter her life. It did receive a very favorable review in the *Southern Literary Messenger*, which called the work a "charming series of sketches" and hailed "the advent of a new Virginia claimant for the honours of literary fame."[81] But, as she had declared in *Silverwood*, Junkin was no longer willing to pay the price for such fame. At the close of 1856 she continued to live in the president's house with her father, Major Jackson, sister Julia, and Julia's new husband, Junius Fishburn, a professor at Washington College.[82] Now thirty-six years old, she set about, with all the disappointment and frustration she had vented in *Silverwood*, to do what was left for her. It was time to get married.

Chapter Four

FAMILY TIES FORMED
AND SEVERED

Divided by War, 1856–1861

John Thomas Lewis Preston was, according to his daughter, Elizabeth Preston Allan, a member of the "old regime which was almost feudal in its relation to women, children and dependants of all kinds. From such he exacted instant and unquestioning obedience."[1] Such a man seems hardly a wise choice for the fiery and independent Margaret Junkin. Yet John Preston had many attributes that Junkin might have found appealing. Born in Lexington in 1811, he hailed from one of Virginia's most prestigious families. His grandfather, Edmund Randolph, was the first U.S. attorney general and the second secretary of state. Preston attended Washington College and Yale. He was an attorney and businessman before becoming a professor of Latin and English at the Virginia Military Institute, a school he had helped to found. Preston was a slaveholder and, like Junkin, active in local colonization efforts. He was also a leader in the Presbyterian Church. While Junkin was surely drawn to many of Preston's intellectual and spiritual qualities, she was probably impressed by his physical presence as well. A handsome man, Preston was six feet tall with blue eyes and gray hair.[2]

Yet romance did not blossom instantly for Junkin and the distinguished professor. In fact John Preston was married when he and Junkin first met. His wife, Sally, was very different from Margaret Junkin. Sally Preston had devoted her life to her husband and their eight children (one of whom died in childhood). But the family was forever changed when Sally died in childbirth on January 4, 1856. John Preston sent his younger children to live with his sister, Elizabeth Preston Cocke, on her James River plantation, Oakland.[3] He no doubt hoped to find a new wife and a mother for his children, so he could bring his children back home to Lexington.

Margaret Junkin was not the most conventional of choices, but John Preston's attraction to her was certainly understandable. Her education, though informal, was comparable to his own, and the two shared several interests. According to his daughter, Major Preston admired Junkin's "intellect, her poetic gift, her artistic skill; he also valued her domestic capabilities, and reverenced her warm piety." Junkin was not as conventionally beautiful as her sister Eleanor had been, but she was a petite woman with curly red hair, who looked far younger that her years.[4] Though he appreciated Junkin's talent, John Preston did not believe that a woman's name should appear in print.[5] These convictions did not dissuade Junkin, since, as *Silverwood* had made clear, she was resigned to the fact that she would never be accepted as a publishing author.

Junkin was not, however, going to submit to all John Preston's "almost feudal" attitudes. Complicating matters, Major Preston had a temper, and Junkin, according to Elizabeth Preston Allan, was "quick-tempered, impulsive, high-spirited" and used to being deferred to by her family. It is not surprising that the courtship was "stormy," to use Elizabeth's term. When Junkin hesitated at the suggestion that they marry on John and Sally Preston's wedding anniversary, August 2, 1857, John Preston stated that they would "not [be married] at all." Junkin, in spite of her loneliness at this point in her life, stood her ground. It was only after George Junkin and Thomas Jackson intervened that the engagement was resumed and a new date set. The pair married on August 3 in the Junkin home, just one day after the original date, with Dr. Junkin officiating.[6]

For their wedding trip the couple traveled to Oakland plantation, where Margaret Preston met her new stepchildren. At least one of the Preston children, eight-year-old Elizabeth, was favorably impressed by her stepmother. "I enthusiastically admired her fine trousseau," she later wrote, "her gold eye-glasses, her pretty auburn curls looped back over her ears, and her gift for story-telling. . . . She was so slight and fair and girlish-looking in her low cut blue silk gown— sky blue, it was called—and wedding pearls, that she might easily have passed for twenty-five, instead of thirty-seven."[7] Margaret Preston was not as charmed. At the sight of Elizabeth and five-year-old John, her "heart sank," she wrote years later. She found them to be "queer little figures . . . in dark calico dresses, [their] hatless heads . . . covered with short, sunburnt hair . . . [their] faces freckled. . . . Did ever a gentleman's children look so forlorn!"[8]

Preston met additional members of her husband's family during her stay at Elizabeth Cocke's plantation. Some of them were skeptical of a woman who had been a publishing author, but she soon won them over. One of the converts was William C. Preston, John Preston's uncle from South Carolina, who declared that

the new bride was "an Encyclopedia in small print."[9] Margaret Preston suc-
ceeded with her in-laws by behaving just as the character of Dora Vincent had
in "The Reconcilement of the Real and the Ideal": she couched her intellect in
her femininity. As Elizabeth Preston later recalled, "She never introduced topics,
or 'lead in conversation,' as literary women were supposed to do. She was the
farthest remove from a pedant, but no matter what her companions were talk-
ing of, they presently found that Mrs. Preston knew more about it than they did
themselves, and would, with a little encouragement, meet them on their own
ground and carry off the honors."[10]

After a month's visit the newlyweds, accompanied by the Preston children,
returned to Lexington, where Margaret Preston's life was dramatically changed.
At thirty-seven years old she was a wife and mother for the first time, the mistress of a large, three-story house, and the primary caregiver for six of her husband's children. She had the assistance of John Preston's household slaves, one
of whom helped to care for the children. She was a positive influence on the children, and she worked on improving their wardrobes, the first sight of which had
so distressed her. The household grew still larger when Preston gave birth to two
sons: George Junkin Preston on July 2, 1858, and Herbert Rush Preston on January 24, 1861.[11]

Within two years of the publication of *Silverwood,* Margaret Junkin Preston
had fulfilled the destiny she had outlined for herself in that novel. She had given
up her writing and had instead pursued those avenues with which Southern
society was comfortable: marriage and motherhood. In John Preston she had
found a man similar to Cleaveland, in that he accepted, even appreciated, her
mastery of the "real" and the "ideal." But the similarities stopped there, because
he, like most of society, did not approve of his wife's name appearing in print.
In her choice of a husband Margaret Preston had committed herself to her decision to give up her writing career.

Preston's marriage also tied her to the state of Virginia at a time when tensions were escalating between the slaveholding and nonslaveholding states.
Abolitionist sentiments were spreading throughout the North, and Southerners,
dependent on slave labor, were afraid that the strengthening abolitionist movement exposed them to violence.[12] Preston was closely associated with two events
in 1859 that seemed to confirm such fears. In April the Junkin household was
allegedly poisoned by two of its slaves. George Junkin, the recently widowed
Julia, and Julia's son were among those who became sick, and arsenic was found
in the supper cream. The two slaves were arraigned before the local court, but,
without conclusive evidence, the case was dismissed. Thankfully everyone living
in the president's house at the time recovered.[13] Of more universal significance
Major Preston accompanied twenty-one of the institute's cadets to Charlestown,

Virginia, in December to serve as military guard for the execution of John Brown. Brown's raid on Harpers Ferry, 150 miles from Lexington, had brought the threat of an armed slave rebellion close to reality.[14]

Major Preston wrote his wife a long letter from Charlestown describing Brown's execution in detail. In it he emphasized the atmosphere of fear and tension that pervaded Virginia during that time. He described the imposing military force the governor had believed was necessary:

> The Cadets were immediately in rear of the gallows, with a howitzer on the right and left, a little behind, so as to sweep the field. . . . They were flanked obliquely by two corps, the Richmond Greys and Company F. . . . Other companies were distributed over the field, amounting in all to perhaps 800 men. The military force was about 1500.
>
> The whole enclosure was lined by cavalry troops, posted as sentinels, with their officers—one on a peerless black horse, and another on a remarkable looking white horse—continually dashing around the enclosure. Outside this enclosure were other companies acting as rangers and scouts. The jail was guarded by several companies of infantry, and pieces of artillery were put in position for defense.[15]

Yet John Preston understood that there was an even greater significance to the execution: "But the moral of the scene was the great point. A sovereign State had been assailed, and she had uttered but a hint, and her sons had hastened to show that they were ready to defend her. . . . So perish all such enemies of Virginia! all such enemies of the Union! all such foes of the human race!"[16] The battle lines were already drawn, and Margaret Preston's husband knew exactly where he stood. If a choice had to be made, the "sovereign State" of Virginia came before the Union.

The battle lines separated Preston's birth family from her new one, while Preston herself remained torn between loyalties.[17] Her father, never one to compromise an opinion, revered the Union above nearly all else. As early as 1843, in his controversial speech before the Synod of Cincinnati, George Junkin had expressed his fear that slavery would destroy the nation. Again, in an 1856 address delivered at Rutgers College, Dr. Junkin had called for the preservation of the Union.[18] To him the national union was an expression of the divine will. There never was, and never could be, any state sovereignty.[19]

In December 1860, after the election of Abraham Lincoln the previous month, South Carolina seceded from the Union. Mississippi, Florida, Alabama, Georgia, Louisiana, and Texas quickly followed. By February 1861 the seceded states had formed the Confederate States of America and elected Jefferson Davis as their president. Lincoln's election had not been enough to prompt Virginia's secession, but Lexington's residents began to debate whether or not their state should join the others. George Junkin and Major Preston openly quarreled over the matter because of Preston's pledge to follow Virginia in whatever course she took. Such sentiments infuriated Dr. Junkin, who—according to Elizabeth Preston—stormed "up and down Mama's [Margaret Preston's] large chamber, fiercely denouncing Father's quiet statement, that his allegiance was due first to Virginia: *in* the Union, he hoped it would be—but Virginia wherever she was, Virginia first and last."[20]

Most of the citizens of Lexington agreed with Major Preston and hoped that a compromise could be reached. The students at the two colleges, however, quickly argued for secession, and George Junkin fought his biggest battles on the Washington College campus.[21] In February, after the first wave of secession and the formation of the Confederacy, Dr. Junkin began to teach his students a course on the Constitution. The course, which contained a detailed analysis of the Articles of Confederation and the Constitutional Convention, was designed, according to Dr. Junkin, to convince the students that "there never existed a State sovereignty; the supreme power is in the States UNITED. . . . The right of secession is a national wrong." The students, much to Dr. Junkin's dismay, grew increasingly impatient with their president's arguments. They called him "Pennsylvania Abolitionist" and wrote "Lincoln Junkin" by his recitation door.[22]

The final showdown between George Junkin and the students began in late March, when some students placed a palmetto flag, a symbol for secession, atop a statue of George Washington. Incensed, Dr. Junkin had the flag removed and brought into his lecture room, but the students later climbed through a window and retrieved it. About a week later the flag was again flying. This time George Junkin set it on fire. As the flag burned, he bellowed, "So perish all efforts to dissolve this glorious Union!"[23]

But sentiment in Lexington and in the rest of Virginia had caught up with the students after Lincoln's April 15 call for troops. Lincoln asked the states that remained in the Union, Virginia included, to furnish a total of 75,000 troops to suppress the rebellion. Virginia was issued a quota of 2,340 men. It was now impossible for the state to remain neutral. On April 16 Virginia governor John Letcher, a native of Lexington, sent a telegram to the Lincoln administration. "The militia of Virginia will not be furnished to the powers at Washington for any such use or purposes as they have in view," he declared, "You have chosen to inaugurate civil war."[24] The next day, as the Virginia Convention prepared to adopt an ordinance of secession, students again hoisted a disunion flag atop the statue. At this point Dr. Junkin informed the faculty of the college that he would resign if the flag were not removed. The faculty, in a meeting later that day, decided to allow the flag to remain. As always George Junkin stood his ground. He resigned the position he had held for more than twelve years. According to the account he wrote just one month later, his final words to his students were, "I never will hear a recitation or deliver a lecture under a rebel flag. The class is dismissed."[25]

The day after his resignation Dr. Junkin prepared to leave Lexington. He sold his property, paid his debts, and, since the railways were already blocked, purchased a carriage. Accompanied by Julia, George Junkin drove the carriage 350 miles, arriving in Philadelphia on May 17.[26] According to legend, Dr. Junkin stopped the carriage at the Potomac River so that he could forever shake the Virginia dust from his horses' hooves. He left behind his first-born daughter, whose intellectual development he had so carefully supervised, and two sons, Ebenezer and William.[27]

The final series of events that took Virginia out of the Union—and George Junkin and Julia Junkin Fishburn out of Virginia—occurred very quickly. Throughout the whole ordeal, Margaret Preston remained uncharacteristically silent. If she voiced an opinion, she would seem to be speaking out against either her husband or her father. Her troubles increased when she lost her husband to the preparations for war. Immediately after President Lincoln's call for troops, Major Preston had become acting superintendent of the Virginia Military Institute. All academic work not related to military affairs was discontinued as the institute prepared its students for battle. By late April, Major Preston was already away from home, serving under his good friend and brother-in-law Thomas Jackson, now a colonel. Jackson, emerging as one of Virginia's brightest military stars, was given the command of Harpers Ferry. Major Preston was his chief of staff.[28] "It is the command of all others which he would most prefer," John Preston wrote his wife about Jackson's new position. "He is a noble fellow, and I rejoice in his success." About a month later, in May 1861, Preston told his wife that he did not know when he would see her again.[29]

At the beginning of the tumultuous times that followed the execution of John Brown, Margaret Preston once again turned to her pen. Perhaps the traumatic events of her life inspired her to seek comfort, or perhaps she would have been drawn back into the literary world regardless. The first work she published after her marriage was an essay on the life and work of Elizabeth Barrett Browning, a seemingly benign topic that one would assume reveals less of the author than an original creation.[30] Yet Preston used the essay as an opportunity to revisit the arguments she had made in "The Reconcilement of the Real and the Ideal." Her decision to bow to convention and give up her writing had proved unsatisfactory, and she resolved again to argue for society to accept women into traditionally male domains. Preston eased into this argument slowly. She began the essay, published in the *Southern Literary Messenger* in February 1860, by keeping Browning within a female context: "Of all the women who have ever written verses, from the days of Sappho, downward, there is no one who has established the claim to the title of *true poet* with more distinctness than Elizabeth Barrett

Browning."[31] Yet a few pages into the essay Preston argued that Browning's intellect was on the level traditionally associated with elite men: "The learning, of which her pages furnish unmistakable proof, the perfect naturalness of her ever-ready classic and scholarly illusions [*sic*] and illustrations, compel a respect which the masculine is slow to yield, except as a matter of chivalry, to one of the opposite sex. Her scholarship is of the most unquestioned character; and just because it is true and profound, even measured by the rule applied to learned men, is she free from all the littleness of pedantry."[32] Browning's work, according to Preston, should be included, and could be favorably judged, within the entire body of literary thought. "We do not see what call we have to grant to intellect a sex," she wrote. "Mrs. Browning's has none, we think."[33]

But Preston also returned to another argument she had made in "The Reconcilement of the Real and the Ideal." This one, rather than liberating women, placed an extra burden on them. Browning, she assured the reader, remained traditionally feminine despite her intellectual capabilities: "It must not be assumed, from what has been said, that we consider Mrs. Browning to be unfeminine in her mental organism. On the contrary, the tenderest, holiest humanities, the sweetest womanliness characterize the whole of her writings."[34] This was the concession that Preston believed intellectual women had to make if they had any chance of gaining acceptance in the South. It had worked for her, to a degree, with her husband and his family, and she renewed her hope that it might work on a larger scale.

In her essay Preston also revealed, though inadvertently, one of the reasons why she so admired Elizabeth Barrett Browning. The similarities between the two women's lives were striking, and Preston surely thought that she had an insight into her subject that others did not. Nearly one-fourth of the essay was devoted to biographical information about Browning because, said Preston, "The *personnel* of an author is a key to the clearer comprehension and fuller appreciation of his writings."[35] Like Preston, Elizabeth Browning had been writing since she was a teenager and had been plagued by ill health throughout much of her life. Both women were youthful looking, with small figures. Both women had been shattered by the untimely death of a brother. According to an account Preston quoted, Browning was "nearly killed" by her loss. She survived by clinging to her writing and to her studies, hiding an edition of Plato from her doctor.[36]

Both Elizabeth Barrett Browning and Margaret Junkin Preston had learned that they needed their writing to work through life's struggles. As the country stood on the brink of civil war, Preston had no idea what would happen, what would become of her birth family and her new one, her home state and her adopted one. She also did not know if she could ever persuade her husband and her society that she should be an author. The Civil War provided her with some of her greatest personal losses—and the realization of her professional dreams.

WIELDING THE PEN

Serving the Cause of Confederate Nationalism, 1861–1865

"Would that I may be able to wield my sword when in battle, as you wield your pen!" John Preston wrote to his wife from Jackson's headquarters on December 23, 1861. "Have you ever thought of the conquests you have made by your pen?"[1] With these words, John Preston, a lieutenant colonel since May, told his wife not only that he approved of her writing for publication, but that he actually encouraged her to do so. Colonel Preston was aware of the growing chorus of female authors in the South.[2] Most of these women were writing Confederate nationalistic works.[3] This writing was socially acceptable, because it served a public cause.[4] Colonel Preston believed that the women were aiding the Confederate nation with their talents and that his wife could do the same.

But in 1861 Margaret Preston was still not entirely devoted to the cause. Her father and sister remained in Philadelphia, and two of her brothers, John and George, Jr., were serving in the Union army. She was torn between her father and her husband and between the state of her birth and her adopted one. But her home was in Virginia, and she had to remain silent about her conflicted feelings. In June 1862, in a diary she had begun two months earlier, she confided: "I feel so lonely and isolated. How I long often to fly to dear Father and Julia for a little while, have a good cry on their bosoms, and then fly back! . . . When I am compelled to hear scorn and loathing predicated of everything *Northern* (as must continually be the case), my heart boils up, and sobs to itself. But I must remain silent."[5]

Yet two months later, on August 2, 1862, Preston resumed her publishing career with a poem that exhibits tremendous devotion to the Confederacy and its war effort, contradicting the innermost feelings she had expressed to her diary. As her husband had informed her seven months earlier, her writing was acceptable if it served the Confederacy. "Dirge for Ashby," which first appeared

in the *Lexington Gazette,* quickly became one of the best-known poems of the
Civil War era, appearing in William Gilmore Simms's 1867 anthology of Southern war poetry published in New York.[6] The poem lamented the June 1862
death of Brigadier General Turner Ashby, killed in the Shenandoah Valley while
commanding Jackson's cavalry. Similar to some of the works Preston had written before moving to Virginia, "Dirge for Ashby" combines the influences of
nationalism—now focused on the Confederacy rather than on the United States
—and romanticism. Preston portrayed Ashby and his troops as both brave and
righteous. In one passage she compared Ashby to the medieval French knight
Chevalier de Bayard (Pierre Terrail, Seigneur de Bayard, circa 1473–1524) the
very prototype of chivalry in romantic thought. She also made reference to
Algernon Sidney and John Hampden, two seventeenth-century figures in the
struggle against monarchical tyranny in England:

> Bold as the lion's heart—
> Dauntlessly brave—
> Knightly as knightliest
> Bayard might crave;
> Sweet, with all Sydney's grace,
> Tender as Hampden's face,
> Who now shall fill the space,
> Void by his grave?[7]

The loss of Ashby, Preston concluded, should encourage the Southern troops to
fight harder. She reminded them that they still had another great hero in their
midst, her brother-in-law, now known as "Stonewall" Jackson:

> Yet, charge as gallantly,
> Ye, whom he led!
> Jackson, the victor, still
> Leads, at your head!
> Heroes! be battle done
> Bravelier, every one
> Nerved by the thought alone—
> Ashby is dead![8]

Margaret Preston, like many Southern women, had learned that her writing
was acceptable if it served the Confederate cause. When her husband, a man she
knew to be very traditional, told her to pick up her pen, he told her to do so
in service of the new nation. Though she was conflicted about the war, Preston contributed to Confederate nationalistic literature because it gave her the
much-welcomed opportunity to resume an active career. Confederate nationalism created a positive change in the sorts of activities men such as John Preston

considered socially acceptable for women. Nationalism provided the means for Preston and other Southern women writers to expand their place.[9] The needs of the new nation outweighed concerns about gender roles.

But the trials of war overshadowed the pride and happiness Preston felt about her resumed career, and her ambivalence about the conflict was exacerbated. In addition to worrying about her Northern relations, Preston spent the war's first year concerned about rising prices and shortages of food and clothing. She was most anxious about the effects of the war on her children. In her diary entry of April 3, 1862, she lamented: "I actually dressed my baby [Herbert] all winter in calico dresses made out of the lining of an old dressing-gown; and G. [George] in clothes concocted out of old castaways." Later, she wrote: "By way of recording the straits to which war-times have reduced matters, let me note that today I made my George a jacket out of a *worn out* old gingham apron! And pants out of an old coat, by piecing the sleeves together."[10]

Preston's greatest concern was for the safety of her husband, who divided his time between Jackson's camp and the Virginia Military Institute. She continually implored him not to return to the battlefront, as she wrote on April 14: "I do not conceive that the indications of Providence point him to go," she observed, "and I have perhaps gone beyond a wife's privilege in my *strenuous* use of arguments to induce him to think so too." Her fears for her husband, who left two weeks later, were intensified when, from her own home, she heard cannonading.[11]

Colonel Preston returned on May 17, but the trials of the household had only begun. That same month, his second son, Frank, had an arm amputated as a result of a battle wound at Winchester, Virginia.[12] On September 3, news came that Willy, the third Preston boy, not even eighteen years of age, had been mortally wounded at the Second Battle of Manassas. The depth of her pain surprised Margaret Preston, who confided to her diary, "I did not know how I loved the dear boy. My heart is wrung with grief. . . . My eyes ache with weeping." The sorrows of war were increasing, and, on the sixth, she exclaimed: "Who thinks of or cares for victory now!"[13]

Willy's father was grief stricken and immediately set out for northern Virginia. He found his boy's remains but was unable to bring them home for a proper burial. This turn of events surely rekindled Preston's heartbreak at her brother Joseph's burial so far away from home. After Colonel Preston's return, his wife wrote that he kept repeating the words, "Slain in battle—Slain in battle."[14] These words inspired Margaret Preston's tribute to Willy:

> Break, my heart, and ease this pain—
> Cease to throb, thou tortured brain;
> Let me die,—since he is slain,
>   —Slain in battle!

. . . .

Not a pillow for his head—
Not a hand to smooth his bed—
Not one tender parting said,
                    —Slain in battle!

Straightway from that bloody sod,
Where the trampling horsemen trod—
Lifted to the arms of God;
                    —Slain in battle.[15]

Just a few months later, Randolph, the fourth son in the family, died of typhoid fever. Christmas at the Preston home was a sad occasion. On Christmas Eve Margaret Preston compared that Christmas to the one before, when neither death nor injury had claimed any member of the immediate family: "*Now* the sadness of the household forbids any recognition of Christmas; we are scattered to our own separate rooms to mourn over the contrast, and the Library is in darkness. Willy, whose genial face rises so brightly before me, lies in a distant grave—cut off by a violent death. Randolph's coffin has been carried out of the house so recently that no sunshine has yet come back. Frank is here with his *one* arm, making me feel perpetually grieved for him."[16]

Preston's personal loyalties were divided by the conflict, and she was not devoted to the war effort. Instead, she wanted the suffering to stop. She did not "think of or care for victory." Yet, again, she published a poem at odds with her most private feelings. Though it acknowledged the suffering the war had brought, "Christmas Carol, for 1862" encouraged the Confederacy to persevere:

There are bright days before us! Who doubts it!—
    Who dare
Talk of failure, subjection, surrender, despair!
The words have the odor of treason—for we
On our sacredest altars have sworn to be free.[17]

By contributing to a Confederate nationalistic literature, Preston had found a way for her writing to be accepted, even appreciated. Whatever her personal troubles, she was not going to sacrifice professional success; it was the one positive change the war had brought into her life.

Having learned firsthand of war's sorrows, Preston was pained to see her own children glorifying the war and treating it as a game. In January 1863 she told her diary: "It is amazing, and sorrowful too, to see how the language, operations, &c. of war are understood and imitated by the children." George, just four-and-a-half years old, played "war" every day. He conducted battles in which he beat "the Yankees" and carried off prisoners, laid his rag dolls in bed and pre-tended they were wounded soldiers, and hobbled about, explaining that he had lost a leg at the Second Battle of Manassas. George would bid his mother a most sincere good-bye, telling her that his furlough was out and he had to return to his regiment. Even little two-year-old Herbert joined the game, "talk[ing] war lingo almost as well as George," according to his mother, and pretending to kill "Lankees."[18]

As Preston's concerns about her own household mounted, she at least re-ceived two bits of reassuring news about her loved ones in the North. On Decem-ber 10, 1862, a letter arrived from her sister Julia, the first since 1861. Julia informed Preston that their father was "well and in good spirits."[19] While Pres-ton was supporting Confederate nationalism through her writing, her father was continuing his attack on secession. In 1863 he published *Political Fallacies: An Examination of the False Assumptions, and Refutation of the Sophistical Reason-ings, Which Have Brought on This Civil War.* The book argued that a basis for state sovereignty could not be found in the history of the United States or the North American colonies. Junkin stated that the North had been wrong in its agitation of the slavery issue, but that this was no justification for secession. Finally he called for a peaceful return to the Union as it was, and he again pro-moted colonization as a solution to the slavery problem.[20] Preston received her second piece of good news on December 18, 1862, the day that Randolph died. A note from Jackson stated that one of his aides had seen her brother John, a Union surgeon, removing the dead from the Fredericksburg battlefield. John sent word through Jackson that all his sister's friends were well.[21]

Jackson had continued to be an important part of Preston's life despite his marriage to Mary Anna Morrison in July 1857. Preston marveled at his new-found fame, but to her "Stonewall" would always be the brother-in-law with whom she had talked for hours at a time, sometimes laughing, sometimes shar-ing heartaches. On May 11, 1863, less than one week after they had heard of Jackson's wounding at the Battle of Chancellorsville, the Prestons wrote the gen-eral, inviting him to recuperate in their home. They learned the following day that he had died before they extended the invitation.[22]

Jackson's death was a terrible blow to Margaret Preston. As she had through-out her life, she struggled with her faith, trying to find solace. She told her diary that Jackson had surely earned his place in heaven, for she had "never . . . known a holier man." She also found comfort in the thought that Jackson was now with her sister Eleanor, whom he had mentioned in his last letter. Nevertheless, Pres-ton could not escape her pain. In a reaction similar to the one precipitated by Willy's death, she cried out for an end to the war, regardless of whom the victor might be: "Who thinks or speaks of victory? The word is scarcely ever heard. Alas! Alas! When is the end to be?"[23]

In her poem about her old friend, "The Shade of the Trees," Preston chose to concentrate on the glories of heaven, just as she had in earlier works.[24] She took her title from what were reportedly Jackson's last recognizable words: "Let us cross over the river, and rest under the shade of the trees":[25]

> Caught the high psalms of ecstatic delight,—
>   Heard the harps harping, like sounding of seas,—
> Watched the earth's assoilèd ones walking in white
>   Under the shade of the trees.
>
> O, was it strange he should pine for release,
>   Touched to the soul with such transports as these,—
> He who so needed the balsam of peace,
>   Under the shade of the trees?
>
> Yea, it was noblest for *him*—it was best,
>   (Questioning naught of our Father's decrees,)
> *There* to pass over the river and rest
>   Under the shade of the trees![26]

Though Preston still could not support the war effort, Jackson's death marked the point at which she began to identify herself as a Southerner. On June 24, 1863, during General Robert E. Lee's invasion of Pennsylvania, she expressed in her diary anger and resentment toward the North: "Hear that Lee's army is invading my native State. Well! Virginia has endured it for more than two years! So I must not think it hard that another State whose troops have been helping to ravage her all this time, should take its turn."[27] Later in the invasion, on July 1, she continued in the same vein: "I trust this army will not be guilty of the outrages which have everywhere characterized the Federal armies in Virginia. It is perhaps well that those who still keep up this terrible war should have some short experience of what war is. But this will not give it to them. The country would have to be overrun for two years before the Pennsylvanians could know what the Virginians know of war."[28]

It had only been one year since Preston confided to her diary the sorrow she felt when she heard words of "scorn and loathing" spoken against "everything *Northern*." Now she was writing words of a similar nature. She even had faith that the Confederate army would behave better than that of the Union though she had friends and family in both. The sorrows Preston had endured over the course of the conflict bound her more closely to those who had faced similar trials, and the anger she felt at the Northern troops caused her to identify herself as a Virginian. By the summer of 1863, though she was still ambivalent about the war itself, Preston identified herself as a Confederate.[29]

Preston's anger at the North grew. In May 1864 Union forces moved into Virginia. While Ulysses S. Grant advanced to Richmond, clashing with Robert E. Lee's Army of Northern Virginia, additional Union troops marched up the Shenandoah Valley. On May 15 Union forces were defeated at the Battle of New Market. Three days later Preston told her diary that she knew the fighting and death would continue. Five cadets from the Virginia Military Institute had been killed at New Market (and five more later died from their wounds). For a while Preston did not know whether her stepson Frank was among them. She also worried about her sister-in-law, Elizabeth Cocke. Fighting had taken place near Cocke's plantation, and she was there alone, her three sons all in the Confederate army. "How do we ever live through such scenes as are daily coming to our notice!" Preston exclaimed. "We will soon have attained 'the zenith point of hope,' or 'the nadir of despair.'"[30]

Union forces under Major General David Hunter soon marched toward Lexington. After a victory at the Battle of Piedmont on June 5, the Union army headed up the Shenandoah Valley toward Charlottesville and Lynchburg, the first time that the upper part of the valley had been invaded. One of Hunter's objectives was to pressure Lee into detaching a force from his army defending Richmond.[31] Another was a result of the Union's new war policy. At the outbreak of the Civil War the dominant military tradition stressed moderation, limiting the damage caused by war as much as possible. As the conflict dragged on, many in the North believed that the war should be fought with a more devastating approach. The appointment in early 1864 of Grant as commander of all Federal armies marked the triumph of this way of thinking. Grant believed that the destructive power of the army should be used to ravage the enemy's countryside, rendering it unable to support life. In this way the enemy was attacked economically as well as militarily.[32] The Shenandoah Valley was a particularly good target, for it produced the meat and grain that fed Lee's Richmond troops. According to many of his own men, Hunter enjoyed this new way of fighting. By mid-July, when Grant ordered Hunter to make the Shenandoah Valley "a desert," Hunter had already started.[33]

Union soldiers "began to pour" into the yard and kitchen of the Preston home on June 11. Colonel Preston had left with the cadets, leaving his wife alone in the house with the children, the slaves, and a wounded cadet. When the soldiers demanded food, she gave them two slices of bacon apiece. Soon, however, they forced her at gunpoint to open the smokehouse. She begged, "by the respect they had for their wives, mothers, and sisters," to leave her and the children a little meat. "They heeded me no more than wild beasts would have done; swore at me; and left me not one piece," she wrote. At the end of the day she was relieved that she had at least kept the soldiers out of the main house.[34]

Preston described the next day, June 12, as "a day I will never forget." She was called downstairs early in the morning by the slaves, who said the soldiers could no longer be kept out of the house. Making their way into the dining room, some of the men began to carry away the china, but a young soldier from Philadelphia stopped them. Even in the midst of such an intimidating scene, Preston stood her ground. "I told them all I was a Northern woman," she wrote in that day's diary entry, "but confessed that I was ashamed of my Northern lineage when I saw them come on such an errand." When the soldiers threatened to burn the house down if she did not let them into the cellar, she told them to go ahead. "One cavalryman told me that if they all talked as I did, they would fire the entire town," Preston wrote. The men managed to break into the cellar, which they ransacked. They also searched Preston's dressing room, and took the family's breakfast, including that of the wounded cadet. "My children were crying for something to eat," wrote Preston; "I had nothing to give them but crackers." Later in the day, one of the overseers came into town and told Preston that every sheep and cow had been slaughtered and the horses taken.[35]

A far greater threat loomed. At nine o'clock that morning, on Hunter's orders, every building connected with the Virginia Military Institute, save for the superintendent's quarters, was burned to the ground. The day before, the troops had plundered the school, taking beds, carpets, cut-velvet chairs, mathematical instruments, stuffed birds, charts, books, papers, arms, and uniforms. The home of former governor of Virginia John Letcher was also burned. Preston was told during the day that Hunter had ordered his men to set fire to all homes belonging to institute professors, and she anticipated the worst.[36]

Even amid such scenes of terror and confusion, Preston and Union soldiers found common ground—her late brother-in-law. One Union soldier asked her for something that belonged to Jackson, while another showed her some leaves he had taken from Jackson's grave.[37] Many Union men and officers made pilgrimages to the general's resting place, and these displays of respect inspired Preston to write "Stonewall Jackson's Grave." The poem appeared in *War Lyrics and Songs of the South,* an anthology published in London in 1866:

> A twelvemonth only since his sword
> Went flashing thro' the battle—
> A twelvemonth only since his ear
> Heard war's last deadly rattle;
> And yet have countless pilgrim feet
> The pilgrim's guerdon paid him,
> And weeping women come to see
> The place where they have laid him.

> Contending armies bring in turn
>   Their meed of praise or honor,
> And Pallas here has paused to bind
>   The cypress wreath upon her.
> It seems a holy sepulchre,
>   Whose sanctities can waken
> Alike the love of friend or foe—
>   Of Christian or of Pagan![38]

Seeing the enemy as "Pagan" had provided Preston with a Confederate identity. Now, as her trials increased, she became devoted to the war effort. During the invasion she first expressed in her diary a strong resolve that the South never surrender regardless of what it had to endure. She recorded a conversation with a Union soldier, in which she told him that there was a "deadly earnestness among our men which would make the last remnant of them fly to our mountain fastnesses and fight like tigers till the last inch of ground was taken from them . . . there *could* be no yielding." The conversation left Preston concerned because the soldier told her that there was no such spirit in the Confederate army.[39]

The Union forces left Lexington on June 14. "As after a storm has passed," Preston wrote two days later, "we go out and look abroad to see the extent of the damage done." Though their home had been spared, the family's losses from the invasion were estimated at thirty thousand dollars.[40] Nevertheless the Prestons were grateful that they had not fared worse. Elizabeth Preston gave her stepmother the credit for getting the family through the crisis: "By her mingled fortitude and ingenuity, and her true kindness wherever she could hope to meet an adequate response, she [Margaret Preston] brought us through a crisis which might well have resulted in fire and flame, in homelessness and disaster."[41]

While earlier she had reacted differently to war's trials, Margaret Preston emerged from the invasion of Lexington devoted to the Confederate war effort. "Our spirits begin to rise already, and we cease to feel subjugated, as we surely did two days ago," she wrote on June 17.[42] She continued to write in the nationalistic genre, emphasizing the righteousness of the Confederate cause and the indignity of surrender. "Hymn to the National Flag" was published in the *Lexington Gazette* on November 2, 1864, and later appeared in the Simms anthology:

> Float aloft thou stainless Banner!
>   Azure cross and field of light:
> Be thy brilliant stars the symbol
>   Of the pure, and true, and right.
> Shelter freedom's holy cause,—
> Liberty and sacred laws:

> Guard the youngest of the nations—
> Keep her virgin honor bright![43]

Another work, "A Christmas Lay for 1864: When the War Is Over," published in the *Gazette* on January 4, 1865, acknowledges the many sacrifices that the men and women of the Confederacy were making. Yet its conclusion urges them to persevere:

> Shall we faint with God above,
> And his strong arm under?
> And the cold world gazing on
> In a maze of wonder?
> No! —with more resistless march—
> More resolved endeavor
> Press we onward—struggle still—
> Fight and win forever![44]

Like her earlier war poems, these works reflected Preston's professional ambitions. Confederate nationalism was still the vehicle through which Preston expanded traditional boundaries. But now her poems reflected her personal feelings, feelings that the invasion had cemented.[45]

Beechenbrook: A Rhyme of the War (1865), the culmination of Preston's nationalistic writing, tells the story of one Southern woman whose devotion to the war effort grows as her sacrifices increase.[46] Preston composed the sixty-four-page epic poem during the winter of 1864–65, after her husband—in Richmond with the institute's cadets—sent his wife a small book titled *Wee Davie* (1864), by Norman Macleod: "I send you a little poem which is making a great stir here in Richmond: it is rather a pretty thing, but you could do something much better in the same line," he wrote in an accompanying letter. Taking up his challenge, Preston decided to tell a story that "present[s] a true picture of these war-times in which we live," as she told her diary.[47] Many of the Southern women publishing during the conflict were writing what one historian has called "women's war narratives." The few women such as Preston, who had published before the war, shifted their concerns from the domestic to the public. While women such as Augusta Jane Evans and Maria McIntosh continued to write novels that could be loosely classified as domestic, their works now included discussions of politics and battles—arenas previously reserved for men.[48] Preston, who had had more success with poetry than with her one novel before the war, remained true to a poetic format though she expanded her work to near book length and addressed the same subject matter as her contemporaries. The eye troubles that had begun when she was twenty-one had worsened over the course of the war, and Preston dictated much of *Beechenbrook* to sixteen-year-old Elizabeth.[49]

Like Preston's other stories, *Beechenbrook* contains many elements from the author's own life. It is the story of Alice Dunbar, whose husband, Douglass, is a colonel in the Confederate army. The couple lives in a cottage named Beechenbrook, located in the Shenandoah Valley. The beginning of the poem finds Alice bidding her husband farewell, as he leaves for the war. The good-bye is difficult for Alice, but she is emboldened by the righteousness of the Southern cause:

> For home, and for children,—for freedom,—for bread,—
> For the house of our God,—for the graves of our dead—
> For leave to exist on the soil of our birth,—
> For everything manhood holds dearest on earth—
> When *these* are the things that we fight for,—dare I
> Hold back my best treasure, with plaint or with sigh?[50]

Preston now believed that the South was continuing the struggle for self-government begun by the American colonists in their revolution against England. Previously, in works such as "Song" and "Kossuth," Preston had identified the United States as the foe of oppression. Now, she named the Confederacy the heir to this tradition:

> The right of self-government, crown of our pride,—
> Sole right that our ancestors won—is denied!
> Shall we tamely resign what our enemy craves?
> No! martyrs we *may* be!—we *cannot* be slaves![51]

As Alice says good-bye to her husband, she urges him never to surrender. Her words, emphasizing the South's lack of responsibility in the conflict, echo those of the heroes in other Southern women's works:[52]

> When we pleaded for peace, every right was denied—
> Every patient petition, turned proudly aside;
> Now God judge betwixt us!—God prosper the right!
> To brave men, there's nothing remains, but to fight.
> I grudge you not, Douglass,—die, rather than yield—
> And like a stern Spartan,—come home on your shield.[53]

Alice, like Margaret Preston, faces increasing trials as the war progresses. Eventually, reflecting real-life events, the Shenandoah Valley is invaded. The Dunbars are not as fortunate as the Prestons, and their home is destroyed:

> Ere now, that the trail of the insolent foe
> Leaves ruin behind it, disastrous and dire,
> And burns thro' our Valley, a pathway of fire,

—Our beautiful home,—as I write it—I weep—
Our beautiful home is a smouldering heap![54]

Immediately thereafter Alice receives news that Douglass has been wounded. She rushes to the hospital, only to find her husband lying on the floor dead.

Alice's first reaction to her husband's death is to wish that she too were dead. (Here, Preston inserted the poem "Slain in Battle," which she had written for Willy.) But soon, just as Preston had done during the invasion, Alice develops a strong resolve not to give up, regardless of the cost. *Beechenbrook* ends with Alice's realization that the Confederate war effort is more important than her own individual sacrifices:

Does the patriot-flame in her heart cease to stir—
Does she feel that the conflict is over for her?
Because the red-war-tide has deluged her o'er—
Has wreaked its wild wrath, and can harm *her* no more,
Does she stand, self-absorbed, on the wreck she has braved,
Nor care if her Country be lost or be saved?
. . . .
By the faith she reposes, Oh! Father, in Thee,
She claims that her glorious South MUST BE FREE![55]

Alice Dunbar's reaction to the Civil War is similar to Margaret Preston's in that both women grew more devoted to the war effort with each sacrifice. Yet Preston's experience was more profound than Alice's. While the heroine of *Beechenbrook* was born in the South, Preston's identity as a Southerner grew from her wartime trials.

Beechenbrook, Preston's ultimate contribution to Confederate nationalism, also represented her greatest professional ambition to date. The Prestons paid for two thousand copies of the poem to be printed by J. W. Randolph in Richmond, but only about fifty copies made it out of Richmond before the fall of the Confederacy.[56] On April 10, 1865, news of Lee's surrender reached Margaret Preston. She cried out in her diary: "Why then all these four years of suffering—of separations—of horror—of blood—of havoc—of awful bereavement! Why these ruined homes—these broken family circles—these scenes of terror that must scathe the brain of those who witnessed them till their dying day! Why is our dear Willy in his uncoffined grave? Why poor Frank to go through life with one arm? Is it wholly and forever in vain? *God only knows!*"[57]

For Margaret Preston and other Southern female authors as well, the Civil War was not "wholly and forever in vain." Confederate nationalism provided the vehicle through which Preston and other women expanded their place. In the Southern war effort Preston had finally found a way to gain acceptance as a publishing author, and so she became devoted to the South and to its war effort in public, while in private she suffered torn loyalties and conflict about the struggle. Eventually the circumstances of the war refashioned Preston's sense of personal identity, and she began to see herself as a Southerner. Shortly thereafter she became dedicated to the Confederate war effort. After the death of the Confederacy, Preston's greatest challenge was to find a new public cause to justify her writing career.

Chapter Six

CONQUERING BY
"FORCE OF THOUGHT"

Toward the Intellectual Emancipation of the South, 1865–1870

After the publication of her novel *Silverwood* (1856), fewer than ten years before the close of the Civil War, Margaret Junkin Preston had anticipated the end of her writing career. But now, in the wake of Southern defeat, one of Preston's chief concerns was the expansion of a career that the war had rejuvenated. Preston had other worries, as Southerners faced the financial and physical devastation brought by defeat and occupation. "I suppose poverty was never so honorable before in the history of the world," wrote Elizabeth Preston Allan, "as in the ex-Confederacy of 1865."[1] The Prestons were more fortunate than many in Lexington.[2] In what remains of Margaret Preston's wartime diary, kept until three months after Lee's surrender, Preston's biggest complaint was the loss of the slaves. The war had done nothing to change her attitude about slaves and the institution of slavery: "A week ago four of our servants were dismissed. Mr. P. thought it best to change, so he sent them away. Anakee has lived with him 25 years; he was grieved to give her up, and she wanted to stay. Old Uncle Young manifested no pleasure at the idea of freedom. It is astonishing how little it seems to affect them; they seem depressed rather than elated."[3]

For the Preston family much about their life returned to normal. Despite the extensive damage it had suffered during the invasion, the Virginia Military Institute reopened in the fall of 1865 with John Preston as one of six faculty members. Classes were held in the one building left unharmed, the superintendent's quarters, and cadets were boarded in private homes throughout Lexington. Washington College also opened its doors that fall, and Frank Preston, living with his father and stepmother, taught Greek there. Also living in the Preston household were Phebe, her younger brother John, and of course George and Herbert. Elizabeth Preston was attending Augusta Female Academy in nearby Staunton.[4]

The end of hostilities allowed Margaret Preston to resume contact with her family and friends in the North. She made her first trip to Philadelphia to visit her father and sister Julia in the fall of 1865 and was relieved to find that no one harbored any resentment. From that time forward, wrote her stepdaughter, "no shadow ever came between her and those loving hearts whose pleasure it was to lavish affectionate kindness upon her."[5] The war had both demonstrated and solidified Preston's intellectual independence from her father, the man who had been the greatest influence of her first thirty-seven years. She was surely grateful for the chance to re-establish contact with him, especially considering his advanced age. On May 20, 1868, at nearly seventy-eight years of age, George Junkin passed away. Julia remained in Philadelphia, and Margaret Preston continued to visit her there.

With her personal life as normal as could be expected, Preston turned her attention to her writing, particularly to *Beechenbrook*. Only about fifty copies had survived the burning of Richmond, and she wanted to republish it. *Beechenbrook* was in keeping with the literature that was popular in the South after Lee's surrender. Poems such as Father Abram J. Ryan's "The Conquered Banner" (1866) reflect the despair of the region. Southerners were fascinated with death, mourning their dead soldiers and dead cause. The Confederate dead became powerful symbols in the postwar South.[6] *Beechenbrook,* which culminates in the demise of Colonel Dunbar, mirrors this trend. Preston even added a dedication to the poem to stress further the themes of death and despair:

> To
> Every Southern Woman,
> Who Has Been
> Widowed by the War,
> I Dedicate This Rhyme,
> Published During the Progress of the Struggle
> And Now Re-Produced—As A
> Faint Memorial of Sufferings,
> Of Which There Can Be
> No Forgetfulness[7]

Preston had difficulty finding a publisher for the new edition of *Beechenbrook*. In the South, as before the war, there were no real publishing houses. There were only printers who occasionally put out books, usually without knowing how to market them. *Silverwood* had been published by a New York house, but, as a result of the war, there were only a few publishers in the North willing to accept books by Southern authors. Many Southerners found friends in Baltimore, where there had been strong sympathy for the Confederacy.[8] It was in that city that Preston found a publisher for *Beechenbrook*.

Beechenbrook: A Rhyme of the War was published in 1866 by Kelly and Piet. Some passages differ slightly from the 1865 edition, but Preston's changes were stylistic and did not alter the content in any way. The 1866 edition of *Beechenbrook* also includes six additional poems by Preston: two sonnets written during the war, "Virginia" and "Jackson"; as well as "Dirge for Ashby," "Stonewall Jackson's Grave," "When the War Is Over: A Christmas Lay" (originally titled "A Christmas Lay for 1864: When the War Is Over"), and "Virginia Capta," dated April 9, 1865—the date of Lee's surrender. "Virginia Capta" is similar to Ryan's immensely popular "Conquered Banner," which Father Ryan wrote within one hour of hearing of the surrender.[9] Both poems express the despair of a defeated South. Preston's "Virginia Capta" is addressed specifically to Virginians, telling them that despite their defeat they should maintain an attitude of proud resignation:

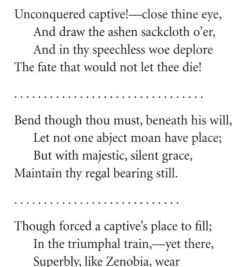

> Unconquered captive!—close thine eye,
>   And draw the ashen sackcloth o'er,
>   And in thy speechless woe deplore
> The fate that would not let thee die!
>
> . . . .
>
> Bend though thou must, beneath his will,
>   Let not one abject moan have place;
>   But with majestic, silent grace,
> Maintain thy regal bearing still.
>
> . . . .
>
> Though forced a captive's place to fill;
>   In the triumphal train,—yet there,
>   Superbly, like Zenobia, wear
> Thy chains,—*Virginia Victrix* still![10]

The 1866 edition of *Beechenbrook* proved popular in the South. According to her stepdaughter, Preston received letters from throughout the region thanking her for "voicing the sorrow and patriotism of her people." Preston also learned that the earlier edition of *Beechenbrook* had found more readers than she realized, for many admirers had copied it by hand.[11] The *Southern Field and Fireside*, which served as a farm and home journal as well as a literary magazine, called *Beechenbrook* an example of the "genius" in the South, adding: "The poem is a very fair reflection of the feelings of our people, both men and women, during the progress of the war."[12]

Yet praise came from the North as well. *Beechenbrook* was favorably reviewed by the *Round Table,* a literary weekly published in New York. The *Round Table* was one of the few Northern magazines willing to print works by Southern writers immediately after the war.[13] Regarding *Beechenbrook,* the journal wrote, "In all respects it is essentially Southern, and in most it is praise-worthy." The *Round Table* went on to say that Preston's poems were "not absolute trash, which is quite an advance on the majority of Southern verse. . . . their merit is even sufficient to dimly foreshadow a time when the sunny South shall achieve intellectual emancipation in a literature of its own, and be no longer dependent on New England for poetry, as well as piety, politics, and prints."[14] These last remarks foreshadowed the new direction in which Preston soon took her career. Confederate nationalism was dead, but she could serve the South by helping it to achieve "intellectual emancipation."

In its review the *Round Table* considered the larger issue of relations between the North and South after the Civil War and concluded that *Beechenbrook* indicated there was reason to be hopeful about the future: "Southern women, we are told, still cherish in their hearts that bitterness of hatred and that stubbornness of rebellion that did so much to prolong the late conflict, and which their husbands and brothers, we believe, have more wisely and nobly dismissed; but if we interpret this volume rightly, if it has not been deftly doctored for the Northern market, we take it as a sign, that, even among the women of the South, at least the more cultivated portion, the right feeling, the true patriotism, is gradually reasserting itself."[15] The *Round Table,* of course, was overstating the case, and Preston surely took issue with its definition of "true patriotism." The *Southern Field and Fireside* came closer to describing Preston's attitude, stating in its review that "Virginia Capta" demonstrates "sublime submission."[16]

The republication of *Beechenbrook* brought Preston more fame and notoriety than she had previously known. Having printed only a few thousand copies at first, Kelly and Piet published a second edition later that year. Ultimately, according to Elizabeth Preston Allan's estimate, seven to eight thousand copies were sold.[17] In 1869 Margaret Preston was featured in James Wood Davidson's *The Living Writers of the South,* with Davidson stating that Preston was "most widely known now as the author of *Beechenbrook,* a poem." Davidson, who became temporary literary editor of the *New York Evening Post* in 1873, was a Southerner who found a degree of hospitality in the North. *The Living Writers of the South* was, in fact, published by a New York house. Davidson quoted extensively from *Beechenbrook,* and included the entirety of "Slain in Battle," the poem written for Willie Preston and inserted into *Beechenbrook.* "None but a genuine artist can thus both create and utter such profound feeling," he concluded.[18] Davidson also discussed *Silverwood,* about which he was not so enthusiastic. "It is not a sensational novel in any sense of that word," he wrote, "and did not succeed in any noisy way, but had a fair success." Demonstrating the breadth of Preston's interests, Davidson also provided quotations from two additional poems, her 1855 translation of "Dies Irae" and a sonnet.[19]

It was not always easy for Margaret Preston to maintain the attitude of "sublime submission" for which the *Southern Field and Fireside* had commended her. In the early years of the Reconstruction period, it looked as if Virginians were to face significant social and political upheaval. On March 2, 1867, by power of the first Congressional Reconstruction Act, the former Confederate states, with the exception of Tennessee, were divided into five military districts and placed under martial law. Virginia, now officially known as "Military District Number 1," was under the command of General John M. Schofield. This Reconstruction Act required the former states to elect, by universal manhood suffrage, delegates to conventions that would draft new state constitutions. In October 1867 Virginia held its election. The Republicans won 72 of the 105 seats at the proposed convention. The overwhelming majority of those Republicans were radical. They supported such measures as the disfranchisement of any man who had supported the Confederacy and the confiscation and redistribution of private property.[20] To a family such as the Prestons, the future looked bleak. Margaret Preston voiced her fears in a poem, "Virginia's Reply to the Vote of October, 1867":

> Confess that thy spirit is broken,
> Sad mother of Heroes!—avow,
> That in present or future, no token
> Of promise remains for thee now:
> All losses,—woe, want, devastation,
> Thy soul in its silence could bear;
> But insult, disgrace, degradation,
> *Must* wring the dumb groan of despair![21]

The new state constitution did not call for property confiscation. It did, however, disfranchise men who had taken an oath to support the United States and subsequently supported the Confederacy. Office-holding requirements were more restrictive; every man who had participated in or aided the rebellion in any way was disqualified from office.[22]

Yet Congressional Reconstruction was relatively short-lived in Virginia. General Schofield proved to be a moderate Republican. He postponed a constitutional referendum in April 1868, giving conservative whites (former Whigs and Democrats) an opportunity to form an alliance with moderate Republicans. This coalition gained control of the governorship and state legislature in an election held on July 6, 1869. The newly elected governor, Gilbert Walker, was a Republican, but the majority of those elected to the legislature were conservatives. The coalition also won most of the state's congressional seats. In this election the voting and office-holding restrictions of the new constitution were rejected. By October, Virginia had approved the Fourteenth and Fifteenth Amendments, and by January 1870 the state had been readmitted into the Union. Thus, Reconstruction in Virginia was relatively short and mild, and the worries of Margaret Preston and many of her peers did not last long.[23]

Another source of comfort for Preston after the war was the presence in Lexington of that great symbol of the Confederacy, Robert E. Lee. Lee moved to the town in 1865 to assume the presidency of Washington College. In "General Lee after the War," an article she wrote in 1889, Preston described how she—and others living in the South—felt about the Confederate general: "It would not be easy, for one who had not been in the midst of it, to realize the enthusiasm that existed among the Southern people for General Lee at the conclusion of the war. Nothing could exceed the veneration and love, the trust and absolute loyalty, which people and soldiery alike had manifested towards him through the struggle. But it was after the war had closed that the affection of the people seemed more than ever a consecrated one."[24]

Preston's connection to Lee actually began before his arrival in Lexington. Immediately after the war, General Lee and his family moved into a vacant plantation owned by Preston's sister-in-law, Elizabeth Cocke. The plantation, called Derwent, adjoined Mrs. Cocke's. Shortly thereafter the board of trustees of Washington College offered Lee the presidency of that institution, scarcely hoping he would accept. But he did accept, and he arrived in Lexington in the summer of 1865.[25]

Though she had had a close relationship with another of the Confederacy's great heroes, "Stonewall" Jackson, and had regarded him as a friend and family member, Preston nevertheless found it difficult to see General Lee as an equal at first. In her 1889 article she described an early meeting with the general. Preston took her son Herbert with her to the house of the college president, where she had lived with her father, in order to pay formal respects to the Lees. As they were leaving, Herbert, then four years old, realized that he had lost his cap. Mrs. Lee, according to Preston, "interrupt[ed] her husband in his animated talk with some distinguished gentlemen . . . to say: 'Robert, Herbert Preston has lost his cap; will you go into the back parlor and see if he has left it there?'" At the time Preston had expected that a servant might be asked to do the errand. "We were not used then to hear the leader of our armies bidden to wait on a child!" she explained.[26]

Preston and the other citizens of Lexington soon grew used to seeing Lee riding about town upon his beloved horse, Traveler, always courteous to passersby and sometimes offering rides to children. His love for children, in fact, became well-known. One Christmas morning, he delivered Christmas presents to George and Herbert Preston as well as to the children of all his other close acquaintances.[27] On another occasion Lee and his daughter Agnes paid a visit to the Preston home. Inquiring about the two little boys of the house, the general was told that they both were ill with the croup and were not allowed to leave their room. The next afternoon, amid stormy weather, Lee reappeared at the Preston doorstep. He had brought a basket of nuts for one of the boys and a picture of a dog for the other.[28]

Another characteristic of Lee's that Lexingtonians quickly acknowledged was his ability to remember a name and a face. Elizabeth Preston was particularly proud when the general recognized her one day in Staunton. He was returning from Washington, D.C., and was preparing to board the stagecoach to Lexington, when he saw the little girl walking across the street with forty-nine schoolmates. Lee crossed the street, called Elizabeth by name, and asked her if he could give any message to her mother and father. Lee's actions were especially impressive, according to Elizabeth Preston, because, not only was she out of the context in which he knew her, but he had spoken with her only once before.[29]

In time Lee was transformed in Margaret Preston's eyes from a beloved symbol into a friend whom she respected and cherished. In "General Lee after the War," she enumerated some of Lee's other traits. She described him as considerate of the feelings of others, humble, deeply religious, and devoted to his family. "There was about him a stately dignity, calm poise, absolute self-possession, entire absence of self-consciousness, and gracious consideration for all about him that made a combination of character not to be surpassed," she wrote. She did not see him as infallible, however, and inferred that the professors at Washington College were sometimes frustrated at his "giving himself up to every detail of college discipline and life."[30]

It was therefore another sad loss in Preston's life when in October 1870 General Lee passed away. She heard of the death while visiting in Philadelphia. Returning home on the twenty-third, she wrote that the churches "are all heavily draped with black.... The whole front of the College and Institute are draped too." On November 7 Preston composed "Gone Forward," a poem dedicated to the general. The poem was based on the phrase "Let the tent be struck," which, Mrs. Lee told Preston, Lee had uttered during his last illness. Preston interpreted the phrase as characteristic of General Lee's "obedience to orders" and "readiness for the duty of advance."[31] She concluded that in life Lee was indeed victorious:

> Yes, "Let the tent be struck:" Victorious morning
>   Through every crevice flashes in a day
> Magnificent beyond all earth's adorning:

The night is over; wherefore should he stay?
And wherefore should our voices choke to say,
    The General has gone forward"?

Life's foughten field not once beheld surrender;
    But with superb endurance, present, past,
Our pure Commander, lofty, simple, tender,
    Through good, through ill, held his high purpose fast,
    Wearing his armor spotless,—till at last,
        Death gave the final, "*Forward.*"[32]

Robert E. Lee was not the only famous Southerner Preston came to cherish after the war. The well-known scientist Matthew F. Maury became connected with the Virginia Military Institute after the conflict, and he and his family moved into one of the homes reserved for the professors. He did not actually teach at the institute but instead worked on a geography book during his time there. Preston, according to her stepdaughter, grew "much attached" to the "warm-hearted old man." During his final illness, she received daily accounts of his condition. After his February 1873 death, as she had with Lee, she wrote a tribute based on some of his last reported words. Preston was told that, when his wife asked whether he wanted to be buried in the Confederate cemetery in Richmond, Maury had replied: "As you please, my dear, but do not carry me through the Pass until the ivy and laurel are in bloom, and you can cover my bier with their beauty." Preston, unable to attend the funeral service, composed "Through the Pass" while her family members were attending the funeral and read it for them on their return.[33] The poem captures the beauty of nature, which Maury loved so well:

"Home,—bear me home, at last,"—he said,
    "And lay me where my dead are lying,
But not while skies are overspread,
    And mournful wintry winds are sighing.

"Wait till the royal march of Spring
    Carpets your mountain fastness over,—
Till chattering birds are on the wing,
    And buzzing bees are in the clover.

"Wait till the laurel bursts its buds,
    And creeping ivy flings its graces
About the lichen'd rocks, and floods
    Of sunshine fill the shady places."[34]

Maury's final wish was granted, and the institute's library served as his resting place until spring.

Another acquaintance Preston made after the war became the most important person in her professional life, though she never actually met him. In January 1868 Preston received a letter from Southern writer Paul Hamilton Hayne. "My Dear Madam," he began, "—For a long time past I have been one of the thousands in our section who read your poetry with sincere pleasure." Hayne went on to praise "Jackson's Grave" for its "true passion" and "noble music." He enclosed one of his own poems, concluding: "a true poet like yourself will comprehend the artistic purpose at once."[35]

It was indeed an honor and a thrill for Margaret Preston to receive such a letter. By this time Paul Hamilton Hayne was becoming known throughout the country as the representative poet of the South.[36] Born in 1830 to a wealthy Charleston family, Hayne had published three volumes of verse before war's outbreak, two of them in the North. He had made the acquaintance of James Russell Lowell, Oliver Wendell Holmes, Henry Wadsworth Longfellow, and other important Northern literary figures. Hayne complained to his Northern friends that his work was not properly appreciated in the South, and he considered moving to Boston. But his personal outlook was decidedly Southern, and when war came, he cast his lot with his homeland. He spent some time in the Confederate army and published poems in Southern newspapers and magazines. At war's end Hayne found himself nearly penniless, his home having been destroyed during the siege of Charleston. With nothing left for him in the city of his birth, he built a small cottage near Augusta, Georgia, where he lived with his wife and son. It was from there that he corresponded with Holmes, Longfellow, John Greenleaf Whittier, and William Cullen Bryant, among others, and from there that he successfully fought to be published again in the North.[37]

The war had provided Hayne's writing with a new purpose. He no longer hoped for proper recognition within his region; rather he longed for his region to be respected in the world. "Overthrown in our efforts to establish a political nationality by *force of arms*," he wrote in September 1866, "we may yet establish an intellectual dynasty more glorious and permanent by *force of thought*."[38] He had selected Margaret Preston as someone he believed could help him with this mission. "Your genius and lofty patriotism have struck me so forcibly," he told her.[39]

Preston replied on February 14, 1868, telling Hayne that she had been too ill to do so earlier: "Your most agreeable note, suggestive of the amenities that ought to be exchanged in the guild of letters, was received some time since; but owing to severe indisposition on my part, I have been unable to acknowledge it, or to tell you what a kindling of pleasure it gave me."[40] She explained that she felt as if she already knew him, being so familiar with him as "one of the South's purest and best singers." Along with her letter, Preston sent Hayne a copy of *Beechenbrook*. She was very modest about that work, stating that it was "dashed off at a few sittings" and intended only for her husband's enjoyment. "I have not cared to take the trouble to improve it much beyond what it originally was," she wrote.[41]

Though she opened her letter by implying that both she and Hayne were members of the "guild of letters," Preston went on to say that she "disclaim[ed] all title to the name of Poet." The reason she gave for her humility was her eyesight. She explained to Hayne that her eyes were fine for common uses but failed her in study and writing. "And so," she concluded, "I say, I do not enter *your* arena, except for pastime, because the odds would be so against me."[42]

As she continued her correspondence with Hayne, however, Preston revealed another source of professional frustration. On July 11, 1869, she explained that the duties she was expected to perform as a woman kept her from her writing. Her impatience with these duties was obvious: "Congratulate yourself, my dear sir, that you are a *man,* and are thus free from the thousand petty housewifely distractions that fill up the life of a wife and mother! . . . How I sigh for such an *al fresco* life as would content itself with water from the spring, and fruit from the trees, and leave one free to devote one's energies to the getting up of intellectual dishes, in which one's better nature might develop and grow strong."[43] In a diary of her daily activities kept in 1868, the work Preston mentioned included cooking and cleaning, varnishing and recovering furniture, sewing, mending the carpets, and entertaining guests.[44]

Preston had expressed to Hayne the same sort of frustration with traditional woman's duties that she had voiced in 1856 in *Silverwood*. Yet, just as she later retreated from such comments in her essay on Elizabeth Barrett Browning, Preston retreated from her words to Hayne. She embraced the assertion she had made in the Browning essay that a woman should be both traditionally feminine and intellectual. Preston had learned that Southern society accepted a woman's performing in the male domain if she served a public good. But it would not accept a woman's rejecting her prescribed role in order to do so. In the very same letter in which she referred to woman's work as "petty housewifely distractions," she wrote: "But I am not going to run a tilt, with Susan Anthony as my compeer, against the existing order of things. I scorn to see a woman, who confesses even to very positive literary proclivities, turn with contempt from, or neglect the proper performance of a simple woman's household duties. Let them come first, by all her love for husband and children; by all her self-respect; and if a margin of time is left, then she may scribble *that* over, to her heart's relief."[45]

Such an apology was not necessary in Hayne's eyes. Preston discovered that she had found in Hayne a male colleague most sympathetic to her struggle to sustain a writing career while fulfilling her expected role. On August 29, 1871, he wrote: "Good Heavens! *What* a picture your words suggest, in regard to the troops of visitors who descend upon you so often in Lexington!! It is absolutely *terrible!* My *wife* declares that *she* especially sympathizes with you upon these household difficulties, and the marvel to *both* of us is, that despite *such* constant drawbacks, such interruptions & material obstacles of every sort, you can nevertheless compose so *frequently,* and compose so *well!*"[46] Yet Hayne's support of Preston went further; he did not believe that she, or any other intellectual female, should be circumscribed by society's dictates. In the spring of 1872 Preston told Hayne that her husband did not like a woman's "rushing into print." Hayne boldly stepped into the fray, commenting, "*There is no sex in genius.*"[47]

John Preston's failure to support his wife's postwar writing career underscored what Margaret Preston already knew—without a public cause such as Confederate nationalism to serve, that career was socially unacceptable. Yet a new public cause was easy to identify. In its review of *Beechenbrook,* the *Round Table* had stated that Preston would be able to help the South achieve its "intellectual emancipation" from New England. Hayne—who had so eloquently written of his hope that his homeland might create an "intellectual dynasty more glorious and permanent" than what could have been achieved by military force —had already asked her to join his cause. Preston had contributed to Confederate nationalism during the war; she would contribute to the cause of Southern literary independence after defeat.

Preston had begun her efforts as early as 1869. On September 13 of that year she wrote to Hayne, reporting that she had received several letters from the editor of the *New Eclectic,* who was "somewhat disheartened in the attempt to maintain a distinctively Southern journal."[48] Originally titled the *Eclectic* and published in Richmond, the journal had been renamed and moved to Baltimore in January 1868.[49] The new owners asked, according to Preston, that she use her influence "among literary friends, writers and others, in arousing some truer interest in their undertaking." Preston told Hayne that she had pledged to contribute to the journal without pay and that she had also agreed to place advertisements on its behalf in her local newspapers. "Now I beg you will speak a good word for them in one of your Georgia papers. . . . If *it* fails, through the inertia and apathy of the Southern people, then farewell to any attempt to sustain a magazine south of Philadelphia."[50] Hayne respected his friend's wishes, and "Daphles," his six-hundred-line narrative poem, appeared in the March 1870 issue.[51] The *New Eclectic* published Preston's tribute to Robert E. Lee, "Gone Forward," in December of that year.[52]

Yet several years later, as she related to Hayne, Margaret Preston knew that her husband remained skeptical about her writing, for the intellectual emancipation of the South was not as urgent or as immediate a cause as the Confederate war effort had been. But Preston was determined to sustain her career. She had learned the boundaries: she could not abandon her household duties, and she should proclaim that she was serving a public cause. In the same September 1869 letter in which she mentioned the *New Eclectic,* Preston referred to her interest in putting together a book of poetry, her first such endeavor. Her words to Hayne illustrate her characteristic humility about her writing, and indicate that he had been, as always, supportive: "Many thanks for your kind wishes in regard to my proposed book of miscellanies. I have taken as yet no steps toward publication, sure anyhow that I am too late for anything earlier than the fall trade. But really the poems (if so I dare name them, for it seems like taking the sacred name of poetry in vain) disappoint and dissatisfy me so much that I doubt their worthiness to be clothed in the garb of print. They have been the mere *toys* of my leisure hours; what business have I then to set them forth *as life-work!*"53

Regardless of whatever doubts she might have had, Preston worked on her poetry collection until March of the following year. In her diary for 1870, she chronicled her efforts. She copied and revised poems she had written in the course of her career, some of them twenty years old. She was sometimes frustrated by the lack of time that she could devote to the project, interrupted so frequently by her household chores. "Surely it is the pursuit of literature under pressure of difficulties," she wrote on February 4. But on March 12 Preston completed her book and sent it to the publisher. "Not a soul has read over mine [her poetry collection] once," she complained to her diary.54

When her book *Old Song and New* arrived on August 27, Preston realized that all of her efforts had been worthwhile. The book embodied not just the dream of the past year, but the struggle of her lifetime: "To *me* the event of the day is the receiving my book, beautifully printed and bound, just according to my wish. The dream of many years is at length realized, and I have now before me a collection of such verses as I have thought it worth while to keep. . . . It is a matter of real satisfaction that I have been able to accomplish what so long ago I had desired, yet hardly hoped to see carried out. May God bless the book!"55 Preston tried to keep her hopes for the critical response to *Old Song and New* in check, but she naturally hoped for its success: "It contains many grains of religious truth; if He will use it to impress such truth, it would be better than any praise earth could bestow. I *know* this; I would desire to *feel* it."56 *Old Song and New* was published in 1870 by the Philadelphia house of J. B. Lippincott. At the time the house was known to be one of the few in the North that was hospitable to Southern writers. The book contains eighty-six poems and sonnets, grouped into five categories: "From Hebrew Story," "From Greek Story," "Ballad and Other Verse," "Sonnets," and "Religious Pieces." Preston's tributes to her mother and brother, "Left Behind" and "The Hallowed Name," are included, as is a much-revised version of her 1842 poem "The Fate of a Rain-Drop," now titled "The Rain-Drop's Fate." Preston's prolific work on behalf of Confederate nationalism is not represented.[57] The dedication expresses humility and assures the reader that the author has not neglected her domestic duties:

> Day-Duty done,—I've idled forth to get
>   An hour's light pastime in the shady lanes,
>   And here and there have pluckt with careless pains,
> These wayside waifs,—sweet brier and violet,
>   And such like simple things that seemed indeed
>   Flowers,—though perhaps, I knew not flower from weed.
>
> . . . .
>
> Upon the open pages of your book,
>   I lay them down:—And if within your eye
>   A little tender mist I may descry,
> Or a sweet sunshine flicker in your look,—
>   Right happy will I be, though all declare
>   No eye but love's could find a violet there.[58]

Preston's first collection of poems also contains two works arguing that women should refrain from writing. Though their conclusions are similar, the two poems are markedly different in tone. The first, "Erinna's Spinning," argues that when a woman tries to operate outside her domain she will damage her womanhood. Preston's resentment about woman's predicament is clear:

> O for the April birth-right of the trees!
> O for the Dryad's scope to sun my thoughts
> Till they unfold in myriad leafiness,
> As now the quickening earth unfolds her blossoms.
>
> But like a frost the nipping voice grates harsh:
> —"Hence with thy tablets, girl! The gods above
> Made thee a woman, formed for household needs,
> For wifely handicraft and ministration.
>
> "Pluck out these climbing fancies from thy thought,
> Poor, weedy things, that ape the fibrous strength
> Of overshadowing man,—only to fail,
> And failing so, to leave thee less a woman.[59]

In "Artist-Work," however, Preston presented herself as all too happy to sacrifice her writing career for the sake of performing the traditionally feminine role. The poem is about a housewife, busy composing a poem, who is interrupted by her husband, who needs buttons sewn on his coat, and by her child, who desires help with his studies. The poem concludes with the woman saying to her child:

> "Come hither, child, and let me kiss all smooth
> Those whimpering lips! They win me back again
> From the inane ambitions I have nursed,
> To graver, holier, purer ministrations
> Than service of art. . . ."[60]

Preston probably wrote "Erinna's Spinning" around 1856, when she was bitterly convinced that women would not be accepted as publishing authors in her lifetime. "Artist-Work" was perhaps written shortly after her marriage and the birth of her first child, before she felt deeply compelled to resume publishing.

In early September, Preston sent Hayne a copy of *Old Song and New*. "I count on your liking them [the poems]," she told him, "for, from what your correspondence as well as your writings reveal to me, I know you to be genial, responsive, sympathetic, and tolerant." She prevailed on Hayne to review the collection for a Southern journal, since it came "from a Southern source," but encouraged him to be impartial: "I crave true, critical handling; not the indiscriminate praise which means nothing: and so trained and judicious a critic as you are, will, I feel sure, award me my honest *pros* and *cons*."[61]

Preston left for Philadelphia on September 20, and Hayne's response, praising the poems in the volume, arrived when she was away. On October 8, John Preston began his own dialogue with Hayne, writing to thank him for his kind words and informing him of his wife's absence. He joined his wife in encouraging Hayne to prepare a review of the collection. Yet John Preston's discomfort with his wife's postwar writing career remained obvious. Fearing that career somehow made her seem less of a woman, his words enshrouded his wife in a cloak of femininity: "For if others, of better culture than myself, recognize in them [the poems] the hand of a true artist, and catch, it may be, tones of sweet music that hardly reach my hebete ears, yet no one can share with me the delight that belongs to the knowledge that the poet is the true reflex of the *woman*. Her choice of subjects is but the explication of her nature. Yes, my little wife is as full of faith and reverence as ever was any daughter of Jerusalem: the Greek hardly excelled her in love for the beautiful: she is as true and trustful as Lady Hildegarde; as simple as a ballad, and intense as a sonnet."[62]

John Preston's concerns were probably somewhat alleviated when the London *Saturday Review* printed a favorable critique of *Old Song and New*. The collection, it stated, was "one of the best volumes of American poetry that have lately appeared," and the poems were "marked by a grave and truly feminine tenderness." The *Saturday Review* concluded by ensuring its readers that Margaret Preston wrote for amusement, her life being devoted to "the womanly cares and pleasures which a large establishment, husband, children, and 'society' force upon her."[63]

Such a review confirmed Margaret Preston's belief that she could be accepted as a publishing author if she continued to display herself as a traditional woman. She knew that she would also have to serve a public cause, and herein lay the greatest value of the review as far as Preston was concerned.[64] *Old Song and New* had received praise not only from a foreign source but an English one. As Hayne later wrote to Preston, acknowledgment from England was particularly valuable, since that country had given the Confederacy no "practical help."[65] To serve the South's intellectual development, to conquer by "force of thought," quoting Hayne, it was necessary to gain the attention and respect of other regions and countries, especially those that had previously seemed to dismiss the South. Preston and Hayne, no doubt, believed that *Old Song and New* had contributed to their cause.

Chapter Seven

"I Think I May Sing"

Struggles for Women and the South, 1870–1877

After the 1870 publication of *Old Song and New,* Margaret Junkin Preston's writing career held more promise than ever before. Her Civil War writings had brought her fame throughout the South, but *Old Song and New* marked the point at which she began to gain recognition in the northern United States as well as in England. In Paul Hamilton Hayne, Preston had found a loyal supporter, a fellow Southern writer whose concerns about their region's literary reputation had led her to a new public cause. Bolstered by her emerging success and her association with Hayne and protected by her carefully cultivated image of a happy housewife serving a cause, Preston displayed a new confidence and assertiveness in her career. She sent copies of *Old Song and New* to such literary figures as Christina Rossetti and Jean Ingelow in London and Anna Warner in New England, initiating an ongoing correspondence with each of them.[1]

In the years following *Old Song and New's* publication, Preston was a regular contributor to *Lippincott's Magazine,* a journal published by the Philadelphia house that had put out her poetry collection. She had successfully established a relationship with one of the few Northern publishers willing to work with Southern writers at the time. In fact, according to one scholar, *Lippincott's* "did more than any other magazine" to encourage writers of the South. Between 1871 and 1875 the works Preston submitted to *Lippincott's* shared similar themes. "Vittoria Colonna to Michael Angelo" (May 1871), "Mona Lisa's Picture" (July 1872), and "Tintoretto's Last Picture" (October 1875) were all, of course, about well-known Italian artists. "Andrea's Mistake" (September 1872) was about a Florentine master who threatened his career by marrying a lower-class widow.[2]

Preston's exposure in *Lippincott's* led to her appearance in other Northern publications. In June 1872 she received a letter from her friend John R. Thompson, who had owned and edited the *Southern Literary Messenger* from 1847 to

1860 and was literary editor of William Cullen Bryant's *New York Evening Post.* Thompson informed Preston that he had printed "Mona Lisa's Picture," "before any other paper in New York had a chance to reproduce it." Thompson was quite complimentary about the poem, stating, "It is exceedingly difficult to put words in the mouth of Leonardo da Vinci that shall seem natural, and at the same time noble; yet you have done it *à merveille.* The poem is eminently dramatic, but nothing of grace has been sacrificed to power or intensity."[3] Preston must have been shocked—and terribly pleased—to hear of her appearance in the *Evening Post.* Nearly three years earlier, in September 1869, she had written to Hayne about Thompson's acceptance of the editorial position at that paper. "Just think of it!" she had exclaimed. "*The Post,* as you need not to be told, has ever been the determined opponent of Southern slavery,—Bryant being a very dignified, but at the same time a very uncompromising Abolitionist."[4]

By 1872 Preston had achieved a measure of success in the North beyond what she could have expected so soon after the war. With a poem titled "Sandringham" she also reached the height of her popularity overseas. The poem's origins were rather inauspicious. In January the editor of *Lippincott's* asked Preston for a "popular poem." She found no inspiration for one full day, but then, while reading an English newspaper, she hit on the idea of commenting on the recent illness of Edward, Prince of Wales. The heir to the British throne had been near death but had recovered. Preston wrote nine or ten verses of "Sandringham" on January 9 "with utmost ease," according to her diary. The next day she finished it and sent it to *Lippincott's.* The poem was never published by *Lippincott's* but made its way into the *Albion,* a New York weekly with pro-English sympathies.[5]

"Sandringham" expresses the concern felt for the prince in Preston's Virginia home and then declares that this concern has been shared throughout the United States:

> Even here, within Sir Walter's Old Dominion,
>> Among Virginian valleys shut away,
> Meeting, we questioned of the last opinion,—
>> "What tidings come from Sandringham to-day?"
>
> Midst the wild rush of our tumultuous cities,
>> Whose billowy tides plunge seething on their way,
> The throb that stirred all hearts, was inmost pity's—
>> "Hope scarcely breathes at Sandringham to-day."[6]

Preston linked her country with the British Empire by referring to the Saint Lawrence River, which runs between Canada and New York:

Along the ice-chained waters of Saint Lawrence,
From fur-wrapt sledge,—on crowded street and quay,—
A flood of eager askings poured their torrents,
—"What latest word from Sandringham to-day?"[7]

She then went on to mention another part of the empire, Australia, and concluded by telling of the joy felt throughout the United Kingdom at the news of
the Prince of Wales's recovery:

In every English home,—by Scottish ingle,—
At Ireland's hearth's;—on lone Welsh mountains gray,
All hearts now with the girdling gladness tingle,
—There's life,—hope,—health, at Sandringham to-day!'[8]

"Sandringham" was a serious departure from the poems Preston had written in
the 1840s and 1850s, which painted England as an oppressor and as the traditional enemy of the United States. At that time Preston was writing in the vein
of American nationalism. But now, working toward the intellectual independence of the South, she took a decidedly different outlook. Recognition, respect,
and support from England were essential if the South was to achieve intellectual
emancipation.

By April 1872 Preston had learned how much her poem had been appreciated in England. On March 29 she received a parcel from the editor of a London
newspaper, the *Cosmopolitan,* which contained a copy of a letter to the editor
written by Alexandra, Princess of Wales. The princess thanked him for publishing "Sandringham." "A feather in my cap," Preston told her diary, "Yet it required
no more effort to write it than to write a letter. I did it almost impromptu."
Around the same time Preston was told that Prime Minister William Gladstone
had mentioned "Sandringham" on the floor of Parliament.[9]

Preston's joy in these prestigious accolades was tempered by a sense that she
did not receive such recognition closer to home. She was achieving success in
England as well as in the northern United States, hoping that she would help the
South. Yet that region's appreciation of her work was fading. In January 1872 she
had written Hayne that "I don't think *three* lines were ever printed in Virginia in
notice of *Old Song and New.* I utterly despair of the Southern Editors lending the
end of their little fingers to the advance of home-literature."[10] As for the success
of "Sandringham," on April 6 she wrote the following in her diary: "*I surely don't
nurse my fame.* Nor does anybody do it for me! Not one notice have I seen
copied from 'The Cosmopolitan.' How this notice of my poem by the Princess
of Wales would have elated me once! Now it is too late for enthusiasms!"[11]

But Preston received sincere encouragement from Hayne. His enthusiasm on
hearing about the reception of "Sandringham" in England was obvious. "I must

lay all my work aside for the moment," he wrote Preston on April 9, "and tell you of the *heartfelt satisfaction experienced* by all the members of my little family!" Hayne told his friend not to despair about the lack of praise from Southern sources. Gladstone's mention of the poem, he contended, was "*alone worth* all the critiques of North & South put together, even if every paper in America had been loud in your praise!" Hayne pledged that he would do whatever he could to see that she received the proper recognition in their region. "This fact [the Princess of Wales having written about "Sandringham"], so pertinent *in itself,* and so honorable to *you,* & to Southern letters, I shall take special pains to have noticed in *every* So *journal,* or *Magazine* I can *possibly* reach, and influence."[12]

Hayne saw the success of "Sandringham" as serving a larger purpose than simply bolstering Preston's professional ego or even than helping the South achieve intellectual independence. The subject matter of "Sandringham," he believed, could have a special effect on the English people: "Perhaps as the Premier [Gladstone] read your beautiful lines, he thought of the years that are gone, of the So Confederacy, struggling, & alone against fearful odds; anxiously casting her eyes across the water for *some* symptom of practical help from *England;* & perhaps too, the idea struck him that the only voice of *genuine sympathy* from this Country, touching the illness of England's 'Crown Prince' came from a Southern quarter, and was emphasised by the passionate sincerity of So genius. I marvel whether some slight pang of *self-reproach* shot thro the Politician's care-hardened bosom, while he pondered over your verses?"[13] Preston's poem could not only contribute to the respect of Southern letters in England but could also contribute to a feeling of loyalty and affection toward the South.

Hayne quickly set about on his mission. Just four days later, on April 13, he wrote the Northern writer and critic Edwin P. Whipple, telling him of the reaction to "Sandringham" in England. He stated that he had persuaded Preston to send Whipple a copy of *Old Song and New,* and asked if Whipple would notice it in his literary column in the *Boston Globe.* "Any evidence of intellectual improvement at the South, especially in *art,* and belles lettres, I like you to see," he concluded.[14]

Despite Hayne's efforts on her behalf, Preston continued to be discouraged with her reception in the South. She was trying to advance the reputation of Southern literature and, by extension, Southern intellectual activity; yet she felt that most of the Southern people were apathetic to the cause. Even those who were not did not seem to appreciate her efforts. In May 1874 she received a painful blow when William Hand Brown, editor of the *Southern Magazine,* rejected several of her poems, stating that they were "unworthy your powers."[15] This rejection was particularly insulting to Preston, because the *Southern Magazine,* formerly the *New Eclectic,* was the journal she had fought to keep afloat not even five years earlier. Preston was further demoralized by the rejection of

Cartoons, a new collection of poetry she had put together, by James R. Osgood, a Boston publisher. The rejections from both Northern and Southern sources— and her belief that her work on behalf of Southern letters was unappreciated— led Preston to confide in Hayne that she was considering "giving up."[16]

Hayne's reaction to Preston's distress was characteristically supportive. He assured her that he understood exactly how she felt and confessed that he too had grown weary of the treatment he received in his own region: "Perhaps *no one* in this country can enter into, comprehend, or more fully appreciate your present condition of feeling, than myself! . . . I have had to endure the sort of mental despondence which proceeds from 'hope deferred,' and an ever strengthening conviction that the Southern writer—particularly, the *Southern* Poet, must be content with only *partial* recognition from the *Litterateurs* of the North, who distrust whatever may 'come out of Nazareth'; while as for the *Southern* public, the sooner he ignores, and dismisses their *very existence* from his mind, the better!"[17] In fact, toward letter's end, Hayne was so angry that he vowed to end his work on behalf of Southern literature: "I frankly confess, that with the *South,* I, as a literary man, have *done* forever! No longer shall I attempt to the utmost verge of my humble ability to sustain her periodicals, extend her knowledge of art, defend her people, vindicate her character!"[18] Hayne was too devoted to the South to keep his pledge, and he and Preston eventually continued their efforts on behalf of the region.[19]

Hayne, as one scholar has pointed out, exaggerated the Southern indifference to his work.[20] Yet he and Preston were working against the trend in Southern literature at the time. By the 1870s poetry was far less popular than the fictional stories being written about life in the South. These stories, termed *local-color fiction,* employed dialect to describe plantation life in Virginia, mountaineers in Tennessee, crackers in Georgia, Creoles in Louisiana, and African Americans throughout the region. This genre brought fame to George Washington Cable and Joel Chandler Harris. Some who continued to write poetry, such as Irwin Russell and Sidney Lanier, experimented in dialect verse.[21]

Preston and Hayne rejected contemporary trends and continued to write in the same romantic tradition as they had before the war. Despite his anger and frustration, Hayne insisted that he and his friend persevere. Hayne reminded Preston of the many obstacles she had overcome, surely referring to her gender, among others, and of the success she had achieved. "Your name is so widely known & respected among the proprietors of Northern Periodicals, that they never hesitate to accept your verses, & to give a material 'quid pro quo,'" he asserted. Hayne continued, telling Preston that she was the "sole female poet of *Southern* birth, whose genius is not utterly unknown" in Europe. (Hayne had forgotten that Preston was originally from Pennsylvania, so closely had she become associated in his mind with Southern literature.) He concluded by proclaiming, "You are a *born Poet;* and a *made Artist;*—write! sing!—you cannot help yourself there; but believe, that despite appearances, you have not thought, or sung, in vain!"[22]

Preston took her friend's advice and found a publisher for *Cartoons* the next year. The poetry collection was published in 1875 by Roberts Brothers, another Boston house. Like *Old Song and New, Cartoons* is divided into sections. "Cartoons from the Life of the Old Masters" includes all but one of the poems she had published in *Lippincott's:* "Mona Lisa's Picture," "Vittoria Colonna to Michael Angelo," and "Tintoretto's Last Painting." "Cartoons from the Life of the Legends" contains tales set in such diverse locales as Italy, Germany, Norway, and England. Finally "Cartoons from the Life of To-day" includes Preston's tributes to Robert E. Lee and "Stonewall" Jackson: "Gone Forward" and "The Shade of the Trees." Also present in this category is "Through the Pass"—her remembrance of Matthew F. Maury—and "Sandringham." In all there are sixty-nine poems in *Cartoons.*[23]

The introductory poem, "The Good of It," describes the journey Preston had recently taken from seriously considering "giving up" to publishing this next volume. Its opening stanzas reveal the question Preston had asked over the past few years and allude to the hurt she felt over her lack of praise from Southerners:

> When any task my hands essay,
> Wherewith to fill the eager day,
> There rises to my thought alway,
>
> This hindering question:—Whence the need
> Of this thy lightly-weighted deed?
> Forego it, and who taketh heed?
>
> Perform it,—who will praise or blame,
> Though it be wrought with purest aim?
> Done or undone, 'tis all the same![24]

"The Good of It" continues in this tone for eleven more stanzas, with Preston at one point calling herself just one "cricket chirping in the grass." But then she abruptly stops:

> —Mock meekness all! There doth not live
> Any so poor but they may give,
> Any so rich but may receive.
>
> . . . .
>
> What then?—If one weak song of mine
> Should yet prevail to bring the shine

> Back o'er some spirit's dull decline,
>
> And for a moment seem to fling
> A flash about its sun-setting,—
> I think (God granting) I may sing.[25]

Preston agreed with Hayne that she should persevere, and she never again questioned her writing career.

One poem in the collection, "Woman's Art," speaks directly of gender discrimination in the arts.[26] Preston was much bolder than she had been in *Old Song and New*. Only one of those poems concludes that it might be acceptable for women to write and then only if they continue to perform their traditionally feminine duties. Until that point this was the public position Preston had considered it necessary to convey. In "Woman's Art" she eschewed all gender roles and cast scorn on men who refuse to acknowledge the artistic talents of women merely because of their gender. The poem is about a female sculptor in sixteenth-century Bologna and the male colleague who spurns her work:

> Her artist-neighbor, refused to see
> Rareness in any work that she,
> A woman, might plan. "A woman's power
> Bends to the sway of the passing hour;
> Achieves, but never creates. The stone
> Of the quarries was meant for men alone,
> Whose genius had gift to shape it: walls
> Of churches, basilicas, palace-halls,
> Only were ample enough to yield
> To limitless skill, the nobler field:
> But woman! . . . a cherry-stone might well
> Hold whatsoever *she* had to tell!"[27]

The woman he speaks of, however, continues her sculpting:

> Misprized and taunted, the maiden's pride
> Would none of the marble thus denied,
> Nor the canvas grudged. Henceforth she wrought
> On the kernel of olive and apricot,
> Marvels of frost-like carvings,—such
> As grew under Benvenuto's touch.[28]

More than three hundred years later, according to the poem, the woman's works are still being enjoyed and the man's are long forgotten. Thus, the passage of time had proven that true artistic talent is more important and enduring than gender roles.

Preston had found more acceptance as a female author during and after the war, but only because she remained traditionally feminine and used a public cause to justify her writing. "Woman's Art" argues that the quality of a woman's work should be judged strictly on its own merits. While the message in the poem is bold, Preston protected herself in certain ways. The poem's setting is far from her own in time and place, and the woman in question practices a different kind of art from Preston's. Preston realized that her society was still not ready for the semi-autobiographical tales she had written before her marriage, tales that are frank in their demands that she be accepted as an author.

Another of Margaret Preston's continuing struggles is evident in *Cartoons* as well. The poem "Prophets of Doubt" argues that the only way individuals can find peace and fulfillment on earth is through a belief in God and the everlasting life he provides. For those who did not have such faith, according to the poem, death "ends the tale at last." This was the fear with which Preston had struggled for much of her life. "Prophets of Doubt" names some of the things other than God in which people place their faith—Man, Nature, Culture—and concludes that these ultimately leave individuals feeling empty:

> What help is here for hearts undone?
> What stay for frantic souls? What hope
> For piercing prayers that wildly grope
> After the peace they have not won,
> Across th' abysmal spaces?—Who
> Implores not some diviner clew
> To lead him to the central sun?[29]

The only thing that would make a person feel whole and secure, said Preston, was an abiding faith in Christ:

> Keep then your sad negations, iced
> With darkness, doubt, and frore despair;
> Bind up your vision, and declare
> That no Evangel has sufficed,
> (Despite the faith of myriads dead,)
> Upon your deviate paths to shed
> The light ye seek: But leave *us* CHRIST![30]

In the past Preston had published religious pieces while privately expressing doubt. But "Prophets of Doubt" is a frank and complex discussion of the struggle with faith and its ultimate resolution, perhaps indicating that Preston herself had finally found some peace.

In August 1878, a few years after the publication of *Cartoons*, Preston took the message in "Prophets of Doubt" to the next level, in a poem titled "Nocturne."

Published in *Lippincott's,* the poem also argues that death should not be feared. Yet "Nocturne" goes further, indicating that death and the afterlife should be happily anticipated:

> There'll come a day when the supremest splendor
> > Of earth or sky or sea,
> Whate'er their miracles, sublime or tender,
> > Will wake no joy in me.
>
> . . . .
>
> There'll come a day—I will not care how passes
> > The cloud across my sight,
> If only, lark-like, from earth's nested grasses,
> > I spring to meet its light.[31]

While Preston's faith was finding solid footing, her home life was rapidly changing. In 1873 Elizabeth Preston married William Allan, a professor at Washington College, and the couple moved to Baltimore, where William became headmaster of a preparatory school. Margaret Preston was closer to Elizabeth than to any of her other stepchildren; in fact, she had dedicated *Cartoons* to her. From 1874 until 1888 Margaret and John Preston spent several months of every summer with the Allans. The fascination the young Elizabeth had felt when first meeting her stepmother had grown into a deep admiration and love. Later in her life Elizabeth Allan wrote and compiled a tribute to her stepmother, *The Life and Letters of Margaret Junkin Preston,* published in 1903. In it Allan called herself "in all respects . . . Mrs. Preston's own child." In 1875, the same year in which *Cartoons* was published, Allan named her first child Margaret Preston Allan.[32]

After Elizabeth married, the only Preston children left in the household were George and Herbert. George entered Washington College, renamed Washington and Lee University, in 1874. In sharp contrast to his mother, he did not prove at first to be a terribly devoted student. After one year, his parents sent him to Hampden-Sydney College, near Farmville, Virginia. George spent two years there, then returned to Lexington to receive his degree from Washington and Lee. He eventually was graduated from the University of Pennsylvania medical school. Herbert's path to intellectual achievement was more direct. He finished Washington and Lee in 1881, and received his law degree from that school in 1884.[33] Though neither of her boys pursued a writing career, Preston certainly impressed upon them her reverence for the learning process.

Throughout her professional and personal struggles, Preston's love for George and Herbert was one of the great constants in her life. It was of course difficult for her when each left home. In a letter to Elizabeth Allan, Preston confessed that she felt "lonely—as I gave up my big boy on Tuesday for Hampden

Sidney. What a reduced family we shall be this winter—I dread to think of it."[34] Even before both boys had moved away, when she was briefly separated from them, Preston composed a poem, "Georgie's and Herbert's Letter," about how she missed her sons:

> I'm longing for you, dears! I pine
> To feel your lips fast kissing mine:
> I often sit and sigh—"If only
> My boys were here to talk and laugh,
> I would not be so still and lonely,
> All thro' the dreamy day—by half!"
> Ah well!—a week or two—and then
> We'll be together again:
> Good-bye; God bless you! Love each other,
> And don't forget the *little mother*.[35]

As her children and stepchildren grew older and left the household, Preston continued her exhaustive household duties. One day in 1877 she wrote Elizabeth that she had "been on the go incessantly" from breakfast until five o'clock in the evening. She had "boiled jelly, pared peaches for preserves, and put up twenty or thirty lbs. of sweet pickle."[36] A quotation she placed in her 1875 diary reminded her that such labor was expected of her:

> What praise was heaped
> On thy good lady, then, who therein reaped
> The just reward of her high housewifery;
> To have her linen, plate, and all things nigh
> When she was far: and not a room but dressed
> As if it had expected such a guest![37]

But underneath these words was a reminder of the work that was most important to her: "By her song those fairest hands / Were comforted in working."[38]

Preston's expanding career provided her comfort from housework; her housework, in turn, made her career possible. By 1875 she had published two poetry collections and was well-represented in Northern literary journals. The reviews for *Cartoons,* like those for *Old Song and New,* were generally quite positive, and the collection went through three printings. Of *Cartoons, Lippincott's* wrote, "Poems of so much vigor as these give fair promise for the future, and deserve more than merely general commendation."[39] She also received attention when Hayne dedicated his most recent poetry collection to her. Hayne published *The Mountain of the Lovers; with Poems of Nature and Tradition* in 1875, the same year in which his friend published *Cartoons.* The poem he wrote for Preston spoke of the bond the two shared despite having never met:

Mine eyes have never gazed in thine,
Our hands are strangers; yet divine
The deathless sympathy which binds
Our hearts and minds![40]

After the publication of *Cartoons,* Preston had the confidence to begin correspondence with writers as well known and respected as Longfellow and Whittier. Both men were already friendly with Hayne; in fact a few years later, during
a trip to the North, the Haynes stayed with Whittier for nearly a week.[41] Preston
sent each writer a copy of *Cartoons.* It was common practice at the time for writers to include pictures of themselves with their correspondence, but Preston
sent Whittier a picture of her home instead, reinforcing her image as a housewife. Whittier's response, in a letter dated November 27, 1875, was that he had
read *Cartoons* "with surprise and pleasure. It is a rare exemplification of poetic
growth." He went on to say that, if he had seen *Cartoons* earlier, he would have
placed "one or two" of the poems in an anthology he had just collected, *Songs of
Three Centuries* (1876). As it was, he informed her, he had included two of her
religious pieces, "Ready" and "A Bird's Ministry." Whittier also congratulated her
regarding the dedication of *The Mountain of the Lovers.*[42]

Longfellow's praise of *Cartoons* was even more encouraging. He wrote Preston on November 23 stating that her poems were "not only full of beauty, but
full of insight and thought and feeling."[43] At the time Longfellow was the most
recognized and popular of American authors. He had already written and published his best-known works: "The Song of Hiawatha" (1855), "The Courtship
of Miles Standish" (1858), and "Paul Revere's Ride" (1863), and his Boston home
had become a regular stop for any writer traveling through the northern United
States.[44] Like Whittier, Longfellow thought of placing some of the pieces in *Cartoons* in an anthology. He informed Preston that he was planning a work titled
Poems of Places (1876–79) and asked her permission to include four of her
poems. The prospect of being represented in a collection that would, in all like-
lihood, receive wide attention must have been very satisfying to Preston, and she
granted the request.[45]

During the first half of the 1870s Preston was involved with literary projects
other than *Cartoons.* In 1872 the Ann Smith Academy, an all-girls school in Lexington, requested a play from Preston. She produced *A May-Night Masque* in
May of that year.[46] Preston was also a prolific reviewer. During one week in
December 1870, Roberts Brothers, the house that published *Cartoons,* sent her
fifteen books. Preston estimated that she wrote forty-six critiques in 1875 alone.[47]
Among her reviews was a favorable one of Hayne's 1872 poetry collection, *Legends and Lyrics,* published in *Southern Magazine.*[48] Reviewing, she confided to
her diary, was "better than making puddings, and so much more agreeable."[49]

In their letters to one another Preston and Hayne informally critiqued the work of others. They enjoyed a relationship in which they could speak far more freely than they could in print. As they were cultivating and nurturing contacts with Northern publishers and writers, they harbored sentiments sure to offend many of those individuals. For instance, on December 15, 1871, Hayne commented on a tribute to Lincoln written by his friend Richard Henry Stoddard: "I see continually between each stanza, a gaudy, coarse, not over cleanly, whiskey drinking, and whiskey smelling Blackguard, elevated by a grotesque *Chance,* (nearly allied to Satan), to the position for which of all others, he was most *unfit;*—and where memory has been *idealised* by Yankee fancy, & Yankee arrogance, in a way, that *would* be ludicrous, were it not *disgusting,* & calculated."[50] As his words indicate, Hayne was a politically unreconstructed Confederate and remained so until his death.[51]

Though they were often frustrated with their region's reception of their work, Preston and Hayne remained ultimately loyal to the South. They continued working toward the goal of Southern intellectual emancipation. Hayne too was involved in Longfellow's *Poems of Places.* The anthology, encompassing thirty-one volumes, was already partially published when Preston wrote Hayne on December 26, 1877. She was worried that their region did not make a strong showing in the collection. "I'm afraid the South will not cut any great figure in Poems of Places," she wrote. "Barring yourself, [Henry] Timrod, and a few occasional singers, here and there, where are *our* Poets?" Preston then went on to express her particular concern: "Our women singers are scarcer still."[52] Longfellow, perhaps the best-connected American literary figure in the world, had chosen a comparatively small number of Southern writers for *Poems of Places.* Preston and Hayne saw that they still had much work ahead of them to elevate the respect afforded Southern literature. Southern female writers, as Preston pointed out, were even further from recognition.

Preston's ultimate goal continued to be the expansion of woman's place; she had found a way to do so by using the model she had outlined in her 1852 short story "The Reconcilement of the Real and the Ideal." In 1877 Preston's faith led her to a different sort of work, which also served to expand woman's place. That year she proposed and organized the Woman's Foreign Missionary Society in the Lexington Presbyterian Church. She was characteristically modest in describing this new venture to Elizabeth Allan on May 5: "We formed a Woman's Foreign Missionary Association this week. I am the president. We merely pledge ourselves for a certain sum every month. I hope it will accomplish something."[53] Woman's foreign missionary societies were rapidly growing in the United States during the 1860s and 1870s. These societies raised money to support missionaries abroad, fought for the right of single women to serve as missionaries, and actively promoted intercultural understanding. Some of the larger societies even

funded and supervised the building of hospitals and schools. Foreign missionary societies therefore provided opportunities for women to engage in public life,
learning and refining political skills, without appearing to violate laws or cus-
toms. The activities of Preston and the other women in these associations were
acceptable because they worked toward a religious goal.[54] Preston remained
involved with the society she had founded for the rest of her life, even when ill
health prevented her from attending meetings. She lived to see her society supporting two missionaries in foreign lands.[55]

As the 1870s came to a close, Margaret Preston had achieved her greatest
professional successes. She had increased the visibility of Southern literature by
establishing herself with Northern writers and publishers and had garnered
respect in England. She was expanding woman's place not only through her
acceptance as a publishing author but through her work with the Woman's Foreign Missionary Society. To all those who knew her, or knew of her, she seemed
to prove what she had argued nearly three decades before: women could perform the "real" work of household duties, and also the "ideal" work of literature.
As Preston reflected on her career in the coming years, she regretted that she had
not had the opportunity to concentrate more on the "ideal." But she never
believed that she was wrong when, in 1852, she concluded that her acceptance
as a female author depended on her continued devotion to the "real."

Chapter Eight

"My Work Is Done"

Final Decades, 1877–1897

As the 1880s dawned, Margaret Junkin Preston had made a prominent place for herself in American literature. Her name appeared "constantly" in Northern periodicals, to quote Hayne, and she was frequently commissioned to write pieces for public occasions.[1] In December 1881 she told Hayne that her fame was almost a burden at times and asked him if his experience was similar: "Does every literary fledgeling who writes a poem or a book, send you the MS. and ask you to put it in shape for the press? Does everybody who wants to get a story published in *Scribner* or *Harper* write and request you to arrange the terms for them? Does every poetling who writes a jingle insist that you shall prepare such book notices as will make it sell forthwith? Do the people who translate send you their MS. to revise? Does everybody ask you for special poems for this, that, and the other public (or private) affair?"[2]

But the demands of fame were often rewarding. Preston was particularly proud to have been asked to contribute to the Edgar Allan Poe Memorial Association festival, held at the New York Academy of Music on April 23, 1877. "I was requested to stand up for Virginia," she told Hayne.[3] Because of Poe's Virginia heritage, Preston had been chosen as a prominent poet from that state. The poem she wrote, "At Last," was somber, its theme that Poe had gone to his grave without proper acknowledgment of his talent. The poem's conclusion indicates that Preston wondered if her talent also would be more appreciated after her death:

> *He is avenged to-night!* No blur is shrouding
> The flames his genius feeds: the wise, and brave,
> And good, and young, and beautiful are crowding
> Around to scatter heart's-ease o'er his grave!

And his Virginia, like a tender mother
　　Who breathes above her errant boy no blame,
Stoops now to kiss his pallid lips, and smother
　　In pride her sorrow, as she names his name.

Could he have only seen in vatic vision
　　The gorgeous pageant present to our eyes,
His soul had known one glimpse of joy elysian:
　　Can we call no man happy till he dies?[4]

It had been three years since Preston had confided in Hayne that she was thinking of "giving up" because she did not feel properly appreciated. Since that time
she had published her second well-received poetry collection and had been
acknowledged by the likes of Longfellow. Perhaps, as she had told her diary in
1872, it really was "too late for enthusiasms." Preston had always felt things
deeply, and she could not shake the rejection she had felt earlier in the decade.

Preston carried on, however, just as Hayne insisted she should. She continued to be a regular contributor to *Lippincott's,* resisting the trend in Southern
literature toward local-color fiction and the use of dialect. In September 1881 she
published a sonnet in *Lippincott's,* the title of which—"An Acorn's Lesson"—
demonstrates that Preston still shared the romantics' inductive reasoning and
wonder at nature's impact on individuals. The acorn, Preston dreamed, would
grow into an oak that would "crown the land," providing "help, shelter, calm-
ness, joy" to all below.[5]

In 1881 Preston's service to Southern literature took the form of an essay
titled "The Literary Profession in the South," published in the *Library Magazine
of American and Foreign Thought.* In the essay she explained why the antebellum
South had not produced as many literary giants as the North and maintained
that the postwar South was going to be the "equal and peer" of the North. Preston argued that genius was "not made a matter of geography" and that Southerners were in no way intellectually inferior to Northerners. Rather, Southerners
in the antebellum period shared a set of beliefs, values, and expectations that differed from those in the North, and that helped to explain the relative lack of literary achievement. Historically, Preston argued, literature had centered around
great cities, but the Southern people had shown a distaste for city life, preferring
to live in the countryside and enjoy outdoor activities. Moreover, while Virginia
and South Carolina had "given tone and character to the educated class" in the
South, those states, she believed, were hampered by their aristocratic heritages,
their residents satisfied to rest on their laurels rather than strive for further
accomplishments. Preston combined her criticism of her adopted region with a
reminder that Virginia was once considered to be an intellectual and cultural

leader; it provided the nation with such figures as Thomas Jefferson and James Madison. Slavery also, according to Preston, had contributed to the problem, because its presence meant that many people were not in the habit of working. Preston believed that all these factors had changed by 1881, and she predicted that Southern letters would flourish.[6]

Preston's account was obviously intended for an audience outside the South. While it blamed Southerners for their comparative lack of literary accomplishment, it vindicated the region at the same time. The South's level of achievement had resulted from a series of choices made by its people: where to live, what to value, which labor system to use. There was nothing inherently inferior about Southerners. Furthermore, Preston complimented the Northern literary establishment, stating that the South's goal was to be its "equal," nothing more.

Preston's writing soon brought her rewards she had never imagined. In September 1883 she received a letter from a woman unknown to her, Sophia Gilman of Maine. Gilman wanted to thank Preston for her writings and told her that they had been a great source of comfort during a recent time of sorrow. Preston was deeply moved that she had meant so much to a stranger and that the stranger would actually reach out to her in this way. "To think that the poems that *would* have utterance . . . should have helped *you* away in Maine!" Preston exclaimed in her reply. With these words the two women began a correspondence that lasted for the rest of Preston's life.[7]

Preston presented herself to Gilman as a woman who had not neglected her household duties, the image she had been careful to convey. Yet she did not portray herself as a happy homemaker, or even a willing one, as she had in poems such as "Artist-Work" in *Old Song and New* and even in her earliest correspondence with Hayne: "I have never given myself up to literature as my life work, being too busy a wife, mother, friend, &c., for that luxury. I have been for many years the mistress of too large a household to be able to command the wide margins of leisure that go to the making of a literary life."[8] At sixty-three years of age Preston was beginning to reflect on her career and to regret some of the choices that she had been compelled to make. Her poems, she told Gilman, were "crowded mainly into some little interval not at the moment filled with other more imperative things."[9] Preston must have realized what she had in common with the antebellum Southerners she had written about in "The Literary Profession in the South." Though her reasons for doing so were different, she too had not worked hard at the "making of a literary life."

Preston also informed Gilman about her history of eye trouble. In late 1881 her eye condition had grown severe once again. Since that time, she told Gilman, she had been under the care of "distinguished oculists."[10] Just as she had when she was in her twenties, she had ceased virtually all reading and writing. Her

husband, John, and son Herbert kept up her correspondence with Hayne, regu-
larly informing him of Preston's condition. In October 1882 Hayne complained
that he had not received a personal letter from Preston in eight to ten months.
He pledged to her that he would keep writing, whether or not she could reply,
in hopes that he might provide her some measure of comfort. "We cannot *bear*
to reflect upon your suffering," Hayne had stated in an earlier letter, referring to
himself and to his wife.[11] By the time she received Sophia Gilman's letter, Preston had begun to write again, employing, she told Gilman, "the grooved apparatus used by the blind." Preston was choked with fear that she might lose her
sight entirely. "I lie hours sometimes on my sofa, not able to do anything, not
even *thinking* in my despondency, only 'eating my own heart,'" she confided.[12]

Preston's fears drew her closer to her husband. Colonel Preston resigned
his professorship at the Virginia Military Institute in 1882, when he was sev-
enty years old. The two "grew more and more dependent upon each other,"
according to Elizabeth Allan; "they were rarely separated for a day."[13] As Margaret Preston was reflecting on her career, she also thought about her marriage.
In "Winter Love. A Wife's Letter" she compared the course of their relationship
to the change of seasons, surmising that they were then in their "winter" years.
The use of the winter analogy in no way implied a sense of coldness, only that
they were nearing an ending, at least on earth. Their love, according to Preston,
was at its peak:

> Dear Heart! You ask if time has changed
>   The love of long ago;
> If summer's flush of love is past—
>   The love we cherished so,
> Because with hand in hand we walk
>   Together in the snow
>
> . . . .
>
> And as my heart in curtained hush
>   Sits wrapped in dreamy bliss
> Beside our Lares-fire and feels
>   The warmth of clasp and kiss—
> I wonder if our summer love
>   Was half so sweet as this![14]

In June 1884 Margaret and John Preston had the opportunity to take a trip
they had been dreaming about for years. They toured Europe with their oldest
son, George, and Margaret's sister Julia. Two of Margaret's brothers, George and
William, and their wives joined the group for part of the trip. Years earlier, in

1877, Margaret Preston had been bitterly disappointed when she and John had canceled a planned tour of Europe with her brother George and part of his family. During the 1884 trip she was keenly aware that she might be experiencing her last opportunity to see Europe before she lost her sight completely.[15]

Preston took in many of the wonders of Europe. The traveling party toured England, Scotland, Switzerland, Germany, Belgium, and France, and did not return until October. Preston saw places about which she had read, studied, and written for nearly her entire life. "Rarely has a traveler taken abroad such accurate knowledge of the places she was to see," Elizabeth Allan later wrote. Indeed, there were many instances in which Preston usurped the authority of tour guides, taking over and leading her group to their proposed destination, astonishing them with her abundant knowledge of the place.[16]

Preston shared her joyous adventure with her friend Hayne. Despite the problems with her sight, she wrote him three letters while on her tour.[17] She did so by using what she called her "blind slate," the "grooved apparatus," she had mentioned to Sophia Gilman. Preston marveled at the immense size of London. With a population of roughly five million people, it was the largest city she had seen in her lifetime—"a perpetual stream of seething humanity," she told Hayne. She stood in awe before the art on display in the National Gallery, paintings by Raphael, Rembrandt van Rijn, and Peter Paul Rubens, among others. Preston was also overcome by the beauty of the Swiss Alps. "Nothing could exceed the exhilaration of our journey through Switzerland," she wrote. She was thrilled with the accommodations they found in most of the "great cities" on the continent, "palatial hotels," as she called them.[18]

But Preston was most deeply moved by the places that were associated with historic figures. "How historic every step in this old land is!" she exclaimed to Hayne. Preston recalled standing beside the tomb of Mary, Queen of Scots, and told of visiting Sir Walter Raleigh's burial place. As she had in many of her poems, Preston echoed the romantics' reverence for medieval times. She told Hayne that she gathered moss from the stone effigy of a "Knight of the Crusades." Preston also recounted going "all over Calvin's haunts" in Geneva. John Calvin had had a special impact on her, as it was his religious philosophy that George Junkin had so strictly followed, the same philosophy that, as she later told her children, had frightened her. She sat in Calvin's chair in his cathedral and visited the house in which he lived and died.[19]

The historic figures especially precious to Preston were those associated with literature. She was so moved at the sight of William Wordsworth's name on his gravestone, she told Hayne, that she cried. She was proud to have sat in William Shakespeare's chair.[20] Preston was particularly affected by Cripplegate Church in London, the place where John Milton, author of *Paradise Lost* (1667), had worshipped before losing his eyesight. She penned a sonnet, "In Cripplegate Church," to commemorate her visit:

> I stand with reverence at the altar-rail
> O'er which the soft rose-window sheds its dyes,
> And looking up, behold in pictured guise
> Its choir of singing cherubs—Heaven's *All Hail*
> Upon each lip, and on each brow a trail
> Of golden hair;—for here the Poet's eyes
> Had rested, dreaming dreams of Paradise,
> As on yon seat he sat, ere yet the veil
> Of blindness had descended.[21]

Preston must surely have wondered if, like Milton, this church was one of her last sights before losing her vision entirely.

Such thoughts were on her mind when she returned home. In her first letter to Hayne after arriving in Lexington, dated October 20, 1884, she sounded almost as if she had made peace with the loss of her sight. She was thankful finally to have seen Europe and delighted with her new memories. "My picture gallery of memory is hung henceforth with glorious frescoes which blindness cannot blot or cause to fade," she wrote. Preston was in a bittersweet mood, happy she had taken the trip but melancholy that it was in the past. "My Golden Summer is over and gone," she said, "and I'll never have such another, as I surely never had such a one before."[22]

Before her trip Preston had told a friend that, because of her eyes, "My work is done."[23] Yet after her return, she began a prolific period in her writing career. She faced difficulty in composing, however, because she had to dictate the works and could not proofread them afterward.[24] Preston began with a series of sketches reflecting on her tour of Europe. Travel books were popular at the time, and on hearing of Preston's project the house of A. D. F. Randolph in New York offered to publish her account.[25] *A Handful of Monographs: Continental and English* was published in 1886. It contains twenty-three vignettes recounting the exploits of the traveling party. Like her letters to Hayne during her trip, the monographs primarily report Preston's reaction to Europe's sights, rather than describing the sights themselves. The book also includes two sonnets—"In Cripplegate Church" and "At St. Oswald's"—and another poem—"An Afternoon at Kenilworth"—all written by Preston. Just as "In Cripplegate Church" is about the place in which Milton worshipped, "At St. Oswald's" is a tribute to Words-worth's church. In "An Afternoon at Kenilworth" Preston fantasized about the history of the town in central England. She placed a sonnet written by her son George, "Alpenglow," in the middle of one of her stories. George had pursued medicine rather than a writing career, but he had felt so moved by the sight of Mont Blanc at sunset that he tried his hand at his mother's craft.[26] His "Alpenglow" was also published in the June 1885 issue of *Lippincott's*.[27]

In 1885 Preston was asked to write a poem for the centennial celebration of Washington and Lee University. *Centennial Poem: 1775–1885*, twenty-five stanzas long, was a thorough tribute to the history of the school and the men associated with it. Preston included General Lee's words of farewell to his troops after his surrender, displaying a sentiment for the Confederacy that is absent from her works intended for Northern audiences. Preston concluded by calling on the university to continue to honor its prestigious heritage:

> Ye will not walk ignoble ways:
> Ye dare not seek unworthy aims:
> Ye cannot do a deed that shames
> These heroes of our holiest days!
> Your oath a Roman oath must be,
> Sworn with a faith that will not yield—
> Sworn on the doubly sacred shield
> Of WASHINGTON and LEE![28]

A few years earlier Preston had referred to Virginia's proud heritage in "The Literary Profession in the South." Her call for the university to honor its past was perhaps intended for the state of Virginia as well, if not for the whole South. *Centennial Poem* was published as a small booklet by G. P. Putnam's Sons of New York that same year.

Preston's reaction to criticisms of the *Centennial Poem* indicated how assertive she had grown regarding her writing career, especially since those criticisms were from her good friend Paul Hamilton Hayne. Hayne published a review of the piece, stating that there were some problems within it. Preston wrote him a personal letter, dated October 6, 1885, demanding to know the exact faults he had found. She defended her poem and told him that she had received "multitudes of letters" giving it the highest praise. Hayne countered with his suggestions. He thought that some of Preston's lines sounded too similar to the words of Ralph Waldo Emerson. He also suggested that Lee's farewell speech lost effect when put into metrical form. Hayne had also found one flaw in the rhyming. He soothed his friend's feelings by telling her that these points were the "*merest trifles*" and that finding them constituted "*hyper* criticism."[29]

The following spring Preston informed Sophia Gilman that she and a friend were gathering together "such poems as I call religious" for publication in one volume. Many of these works had been published in her earlier collections or in journals.[30] *For Love's Sake: Poems of Faith and Comfort* was published in 1886 by A. D. F. Randolph, the house that had also put out *A Handful of Monographs*. *For Love's Sake* contains fifty-seven poems and is dedicated to Preston's only surviving sister, Julia Junkin Fishburn.[31] Preston's decision to republish many of her religious pieces probably resulted from the strong faith that she had finally found within herself.

During this phase of her career Preston also began to record her knowledge of, and relationships with, the two great heroes and symbols of the Confederacy, "Stonewall" Jackson and Robert E. Lee. In doing so she not only told a part of her own life story, but she contributed to the cult of the Lost Cause. Once Reconstruction was over, Southern writers focused less on defeat and instead began to memorialize and celebrate the Old South. But the Lost Cause was something more than a cultural trend—it was a way to transform military defeat into social victory. Conditions in the prewar South were portrayed as idyllic and the Confederacy's cause as righteous.[32] By giving firsthand accounts of Jackson and Lee as extremely good men, Preston contributed to the Lost Cause and also identified a new public cause she could serve through her writing.[33] In October 1886 Preston's "Personal Reminiscences of Stonewall Jackson" appeared in the *Century Illustrated Monthly Magazine*. She explained the special perspective she brought to the story of the great general: "Knowing him as I did, and having the opportunity of witnessing his daily life in my father's home, I held a key to his character, possessed, I verily believe, by none about him." Preston's essay concentrates on the years she knew Jackson best, from his marriage to Eleanor in 1853 to his second marriage in 1857. She also repeated tales he had told her about his stint in the Mexican War and stories from her husband's service with him during the Civil War. Preston portrayed Jackson as a brave and deeply principled man who also had a sense of humor. She poked fun at him a bit as well, mostly in regard to his strong convictions in keeping the sabbath holy. According to Preston, Jackson would wait to mail a letter until he was certain it would not be traveling on a Sunday.[34]

"General Lee after the War," which appeared in *Century* in June 1889, did not display the same easy familiarity. But Preston was acquainted with Lee on a personal level and could provide a firsthand insight: "Living near General Lee as I did, from 1865 till his death, in 1870, I was cognizant of many little instances and scenes which illustrate this feeling [the love Southerners felt for Lee], and also serve to bring out some of the finer points of his character in a way no stately biography would condescend to do."[35] The essay was similar to "Personal Reminiscences of Stonewall Jackson" in that it concentrated on the years Preston knew her subject best, from 1865, when the Confederate leader moved to Lexington, to 1870, when he died.

In 1887 Preston published her last poetry collection. *Colonial Ballads, Sonnets and Other Verse* contains more than one hundred works. Fourteen poems are based on pre-Revolutionary themes, with titles such as "The Last Meeting of Pocahontas and the Great Captain" and "The First Proclamation of Miles Standish." The subject matter of the remaining works is varied. "At Last," the Poe tribute, is included, as is "In Cripplegate Church," which was originally published in *A Handful of Monographs.*[36]

Preston's sense of her own mortality was heightened by the death of Paul Hamilton Hayne on July 6, 1886. Since 1867 the two had exchanged more than three hundred letters. Hayne was one of the few people, perhaps the only person, to tell Preston that "there is no sex in genius." In him, she had found a confidant who understood her struggle to be accepted as a female author. He had commiserated with her about the household duties she felt bound to fulfill. The loss was compounded by shock, for Preston had not expected Hayne to die when he did. Preston's last letter to the Hayne household was written to Mrs. Hayne on June 24, 1886. Preston knew that her old friend was ill, but did not believe him to be fatally so. She lamented that she had never seen the Haynes in person, and suggested that her health would likely be the reason she never would: "If the meeting doesn't come soon, I fear I shall be too blind to see you," she wrote.[37] Just days later, Hayne was dead; Preston had never seen the face of one of the most important people in her life.

Hayne's death ironically freed Margaret Preston to experiment with new writing techniques. By 1885 local-color fiction was at the peak of its popularity in the South, and Preston had finally developed an interest in it.[38] In December of that year she had written Hayne, asking his opinion of the work of Mary N. Murfree. Murfree, who often used the pseudonym Charles Egbert Craddock, was the author of well-known stories using the dialect of the Tennessee mountains. Hayne responded that his wife and son were fond of Murfree's work, but that he had not yet read any of it.[39] This polite dismissiveness no doubt discouraged Preston, because of her symbiotic professional relationship with Hayne.

In October 1889, shortly after Hayne's death, Preston published a short story in the local-color genre. "Aunt Dorothy's Funeral" is set on an antebellum Virginia plantation named Hazlecroft.[40] Plantation fiction was a popular segment of the local-color movement in the 1870s and 1880s. It perpetuated positive memories of the Old South, for life on the plantation was viewed from a sentimental rather than a critical angle. The Northern reading public was receptive to this sort of literature once slavery had been abolished.[41] Preston, like other writers, used the dialect of the slaves who lived and worked on Hazlecroft. As "Aunt Dorothy's Funeral" opens, Dorothy Clayborne, Hazlecroft's owner, is believed to be dying. The plantation's one hundred slaves pray for her recovery.

"She dun ben a good mistis ter all we," says Uncle Reuben, the slave preacher. The slaves' prayers are answered, and Dorothy Clayborne recovers in time to see her son Lucien marry his distant cousin Annis Fontaine.[42] Originally published in *Harper's New Monthly Magazine,* the story later appeared in book form, a common progression at the time for this sort of Southern fiction.[43]

With an eye to her place in history, Preston granted an interview to Laura C. Holloway of the *Washington Post* in 1888. Until that time Preston had avoided publicity, having, in Holloway's words, "successfully escaped the interviewer and the newspaper illustrator." Holloway described Preston as having a short physique and being "inclined to stoutness." Her auburn hair was "thickly sprinkled with gray." Preston's carefully cultivated image of the devoted homemaker, an image designed to shield her from attacks on her literary proclivities, was fully on display, as Holloway called her subject a "model housekeeper." According to Holloway, Preston was "one of the really famous American authors of the day." In Holloway's eyes at least, Preston had earned the respect and admiration she craved from the Southern people: "For what she has done in literature she is world-famed, for what she has done for the advancement of the literary South, she is beloved by a people quick to appreciate kindness and chivalric toward those who advance sectional prestige. . . . Go to her home to know Mrs. Preston; there you will find her enthroned as a queen, and swaying a mighty sceptre over the hearts of a people who know her well and love her loyally."[44] Holloway recounted the highlights of Preston's career, and described her personal life at the time of the interview: "Her family circle is limited to herself and her husband, and her home is the abode of comfort and luxury. . . . It is the scene of many pleasant reunions and quiet entertainments, and about her gather a delightful and cultivated circle of people, including the faculty and friends of the University."[45]

But the comfort to which Laura Holloway referred was shattered on July 15, 1890, when John Preston died. His was, according to his daughter, a "peaceful" death, after several weeks of illness. Margaret Preston's grief was compounded by the subsequent loss of her home and most of its contents.[46] According to the provisions of her husband's will, all his possessions, including even the household items, were to be divided equally among his heirs. In order to comply with these wishes, the executors of the will—Thomas Preston, John Preston's son by his first wife, and Herbert Preston, his son by Margaret—sold the house in which Margaret Preston had lived for more than thirty years. The contents were divided according to Colonel Preston's wishes.[47]

Margaret Preston had planned to buy a house in Baltimore, where both her sons lived with their families. But the loss of her home "proved too much of an added sorrow," she told Sophia Gilman in a letter dated January 13, 1891, and resulted in what she called a spell of "nervous illness." Unable to walk, Preston moved into the home of Elizabeth Allan. Allan had brought her children to Lexington the year before, after the death of her own husband. "I am unequal to housekeeping now, and probably shall never have a home of my own again," Preston told Gilman.[48] Indeed, according to Allan, her stepmother never walked again, "except to take a few steps across the floor with a crutch or cane, and leaning on a strong arm." In addition Preston, like her mother before her, had become increasingly deaf. While she was living with her stepdaughter, she needed the constant assistance of a long ear trumpet.[49]

Even with these misfortunes Margaret Preston did not leave the literary world. For about a year after her husband's death, she declined invitations to write. Most notable was her May 1891 refusal to write a poem to be read at the unveiling of a statue honoring "Stonewall" Jackson.[50] But by November, Preston was well enough to compose "Giving Children Right Impressions of Death," an essay published in the *Sunday School Times.* In the essay Preston recalled the way in which her father had introduced her to the subject—by showing her, at six years old and without warning, the dead body of a fifteen-year-old boy. This had caused her decades-long struggle with the fear of death; Preston wrote that she still could not look at a dead body. Preston contrasted her father's method with that of her boys' "mammy," who took George and Herbert to look at many dead bodies, soothing them and explaining that the individuals had gone to heaven. As a result, according to Preston, her sons had never feared death.[51] "Giving Children Right Impressions of Death" was surely inspired by the death of John Preston and by George and Herbert's reaction to that event.

During the final weeks of 1892 Preston moved into the Baltimore home of her son George, his wife, and their two children, George and Margaret. Here she spent the remainder of her days, surrounded by family, including Herbert, who visited every day. Strangers came to meet this famous author, but Preston did not feel like making new acquaintances. She was thankful to be near her loved ones; yet she much preferred a small-town existence, as she wrote a friend shortly after her move: "In my old room at Elizabeth Allan's, I looked out upon a range of most beautiful mountains, of great stretches of woodland and green pastures. Here my large airy room faces brick walls and housetops, and when I sit at the library windows, I only see throngs of passers-by, all of whom are strangers to me."[52] The city brought one unexpected gift into Preston's life. Julia Junkin McCay Buchanan, the daughter of Charles McCay and namesake of Preston's mother, lived near George Preston. Charles McCay had been Preston's dear friend and tutor at the Manual Labor Academy and Lafayette College and probably her first love. Julia became a daily companion to Preston.[53] In a sense Preston's life had come full circle, and it must have been a joy to be reminded of the days of her youth, when she was just beginning her studies and discovering her love of writing.

On March 27, 1897, Julia Buchanan wrote Sophia Gilman, to inform her that Margaret Preston was dying. "I hate to think of the future without her," she said, "though her most loving friend could not desire for her a longer life."[54] Preston's "blessedly gentle departure," as Elizabeth Allan termed it, occurred two days later. Preston left this world exactly as she had hoped she would. A few years earlier, in the poem "Euthanasia," she had described the best way to die:

> With faces the dearest in sight,
>   With a kiss on the lips I love best,
> To whisper a tender "Good-night,"
>   And pass to my pillow of rest.
>
> To kneel, all my service complete,
>   All duties accomplished—and then
> To finish my orisons sweet
>   With a trustful and joyous "Amen."
>
> . . . .
>
> Just so would I choose to depart,
>   Just so let the summons be given;
> A quiver—a pause of the heart—
>   A vision of angels—then Heaven![55]

Margaret Junkin Preston's "service" was indeed "complete." Though she was referring to her service of her lord, she had also served the Confederacy, the postbellum South, and millions of women who lived during and after her lifetime. Her work was finally done.

Conclusion

Margaret Junkin Preston was laid to rest beside her husband in the Stonewall Jackson Memorial Cemetery in Lexington, Virginia. The Preston family plot is just a few steps from that of the Junkin family, where Margaret Preston's mother and sister Eleanor were buried immediately after their deaths. In 1925 family members brought the remains of George Junkin and his youngest daughter, Julia, to the Junkin plot.[1] Jackson lies just a bit beyond the Junkins. In death the family so divided by the Civil War has been reunited. Margaret Junkin Preston's epitaph, chosen by her sons, George and Herbert, refers to the connection between the war and their mother's writing career:

> HER SONG CHEERED THE HEARTS
> OF THE SOUTHERN PEOPLE IN THE
> HOUR OF THEIR DEEPEST DISTRESS.

Even immediately after her death, it was obvious that Preston's writing had served the public. More than one century later, the true significance of Margaret Junkin Preston's career—and of why she used that career to serve a public cause—is clear. Preston played an active role in the continuing march of American women toward full equality with their male counterparts. She successfully challenged the barriers against female authorship in the South by redefining womanhood and the purpose of her writing. She began with "The Reconcilement of the Real and the Ideal" (1852), in which she argued that women could master both the male and female domains. Junkin hoped that women would be accepted as intellectual if they continued to perform their traditional female functions.

Yet about three years later—increasingly lonely and isolated and believing that "reconcilement" was not possible—Junkin explored another definition of womanhood. In "The Child of Song" she asked if a woman could be accepted as a publishing author if her home were bare. Without a husband and children, she reasoned, a woman would not be neglecting any duties. This approach also proved inadequate, and in 1856 Junkin announced the end of her struggle in her novel *Silverwood*. She hoped for woman's "regeneration," she wrote, in the future. But in the meantime she grudgingly accepted "the barriers just where they are." Shortly thereafter Junkin married a man who did not approve of females appearing in print.

But in December 1861 John Preston asked his wife to pick up her pen. He and other Southerners encouraged women to write so that they could serve the Confederate war effort. Margaret Preston had found the key to her social acceptance—the service of a public cause—and she wrote in the vein of Confederate nationalism even when her loyalties were divided. In the decades after the war Preston fought to maintain her expanded boundaries. She used her writing to serve two public causes, the intellectual emancipation of the South and the Lost Cause. Yet she also retreated from her words in *Silverwood* and embraced the traditional female role. She perpetuated the image of a happy housewife while aggressively pursuing a publishing career. Preston had realized the necessity of the definition of womanhood she had put forth in "The Reconcilement of the Real and the Ideal." A woman would have to master both the "real" and the "ideal"—and serve a public cause—in order to be accepted as a publishing author. These were burdens that men did not have to carry, but the barriers had been broken. Future generations of Southern women could establish and work toward their own ideal.

ABBREVIATIONS

All items listed below are located in Special Collections, Leyburn Library, Washington and Lee University.

Notebook I
A notebook of original poems handwritten by Margaret Junkin between June 1837 and May 1840. Junkin numbered the pages herself.

Notebook II
A notebook containing works Junkin wrote from June 1840 through August 1850. Pagination has been added.

Scrapbook I
A 34-page scrapbook kept by Junkin that includes her published poems and stories from the 1840s and the 1850s. Pagination has been added.

Scrapbook II
A 148-page scrapbook of clippings from 1839 to 1865. Pagination has been added.

Scrapbook III
A 133-page scrapbook of clippings from the 1870s to the 1890s. Pagination has been added.

Sketchbook
A sketchbook containing drawings and watercolors by Margaret Junkin as well as two watercolors by Eleanor Junkin. The few dated items indicate that the sketchbook was maintained in the 1840s.

Notes

Unless otherwise stated, notes referring to Margaret Junkin Preston as author will use her last name at the time of publication or composition (Junkin or Preston). Notes citing works by others with the name Junkin or Preston will include their full names.

Preface

1. Scrapbook I, 5. This quotation and the short story in which it is found are discussed further in chapter 3.

2. Fox-Genovese, *Within the Plantation Household,* quotation from 29.

3. Ibid., 194, 256.

4. Ibid., 246.

5. Rable, *Civil Wars,* quotations from 113, 287, 274.

6. Faust, *Mothers of Invention,* quotation from 254.

7. Clinton, *Tara Revisited,* quotation from 79.

8. Baym, *Woman's Fiction;* Coultrap-McQuin, *Doing Literary Business;* Kelley, *Private Woman, Public Stage;* Moss, *Domestic Novelists in the Old South;* Cox, *Dixie's Daughters;* and Gardner, *Blood and Irony.*

9. Rable, *Civil Wars,* 283.

10. Faust, *Mothers of Invention,* 238. Preston's words were actually "Who thinks of or cares for victory now!"

11. Blair, *Virginia's Private War.*

12. Allan, ed., *The Life and Letters of Margaret Junkin Preston;* Coulling, *Margaret Junkin Preston.*

Chapter 1—Lessons Learned

1. Allan, ed., *Life and Letters,* 5–6; Malone, ed., *Dictionary of American Biography,* 10:249.

2. Allan, ed., *Life and Letters,* 5–6; Coulling, *Margaret Junkin Preston,* 7–8.

3. Allan, ed., *Life and Letters,* 3. Most likely the "persecution" that the family spoke of was Charles I's attempts in the 1630s to impose his religious views on Calvinists in Scotland.

4. Malone, ed., *Dictionary of American Biography,* 10:248.

5. Allan, ed., *Life and Letters*, 3. The siege of Londonderry occurred in Northern Ireland in 1689–90. Forces loyal to the Catholic king James II, ousted during the so-called Glorious Revolution of 1688, were finally defeated by King William III's forces at the Battle of the Boyne. For the story to be truthful Margaret Junkin's great-grandmother would have to have been extremely young during the siege and relatively old when Junkin's grandfather was born. Whether accurate or not, it is a story that Junkin evidently believed. (She repeated it to her stepdaughter.) It was one of the formative influences of her childhood.

6. Crenshaw, *General Lee's College*, 112.

7. Ibid.

8. Allan, ed., *Life and Letters*, 3–4; Malone, ed., *Dictionary of American Biography*, 10:248–49.

9. Malone, ed., *Dictionary of American Biography*, 10:249; Skillman, *The Biography of a College*, 1:51.

10. Malone, ed., *Dictionary of American Biography*, 10:249.

11. George Junkin, *A Treatise on Justification*, 102, 129, 155, 173.

12. Ahlstrom, *A Religious History of the American People*, 466.

13. Allan, ed., *Life and Letters*, 19–20, 11, quotation from 19.

14. Preston, "Giving Children Right Impressions of Death," 707–8, quotation from 707.

15. Ibid., 707. Laderman, *The Sacred Remains*, describes changing attitudes about corpses in nineteenth-century American society. Laderman's work is one example of the increasing scholarship in the cultural history of death. See also Isenberg and Burstein, eds., *Mortal Remains*, for a sampling of the variety of topics and sources. George Junkin seems to have wanted to help young Margaret accept death as a part of everyday life, but he obviously was not successful.

16. See, for example, Kelley, *Private Woman, Public Stage*, 62.

17. Pease and Pease, *Ladies, Women, and Wenches*, 2, 75, 7–8, 65. See also O'Brien, *Conjectures of Order*, 263–64.

18. Coulling, *Margaret Junkin Preston*, 8–10, 4; Allan, ed., *Life and Letters*, 7–8.

19. Hubbell, *The South in American Literature*, 617.

20. Allan, ed., *Life and Letters*, 8, 16; Starr, ed., *Dictionary of American Biography*, 15:204.

21. Coulling, *Margaret Junkin Preston*, 9–10; Allan, ed., *Life and Letters*, 14–15.

22. See Notebook I, 134–35, for a poem Junkin wrote to her sister, chronicling their childhood activities and illustrating how close they were.

23. Skillman, *Biography of a College*, 1:50–51. Denominational colleges such as this (and Lafayette College in Easton, Pennsylvania, where George Junkin later served) began to multiply in the 1820s. The traditional (pre-1970) view of these schools was that they were products of competition among denominations and not especially useful as educational facilities. But historians such as Colin B. Burke, David B. Potts, and Marilyn Tobias, among others, have recently argued that such schools were less denominational than once thought. These historians believe that denominational colleges arose to meet the needs of a decentralized, rural society. They acted as local institutions, serving the educational and economic requirements of the community, which in return contributed much to their support. See, for example, Burke, *American Collegiate Populations*; Potts, *Baptist Colleges in the Development of American Society*; and Tobias, *Old Dartmouth on*

Trial. For an especially informative collection of the new scholarship, see Geiger, ed., *The American College in the Nineteenth Century.*

24. Allan, ed., *Life and Letters,* 9; Skillman, *Biography of a College,* 1:60.

25. Coulling, *Margaret Junkin Preston,* 21–22. For those individuals to whom Junkin relayed the story, see, for example, Pickett, *Literary Hearthstones of Dixie,* 258.

26. Skillman, *Biography of a College,* 1:52–53.

27. Malone, ed., *Dictionary of American Biography,* 10:249.

28. Ahlstrom, *Religious History,* 464–66, 79.

29. Hatch, *The Democratization of American Christianity,* 201; Ahlstrom, *Religious History,* 466.

30. Ahlstrom, *Religious History,* 467.

31. *Trial of the Rev. Albert Barnes,* appendix 1; Ahlstrom, *Religious History,* 467.

32. *Trial of the Rev. Albert Barnes,* 1, iii.

33. Ibid., 104, 285.

34. Ahlstrom, *Religious History,* 467–68.

35. Skillman, *Biography of a College,* 1:53–54, 58–61; Allan, ed., *Life and Letters,* 10.

36. Coulling, *Margaret Junkin Preston,* 24.

Chapter 2—An American Female Poet

1. Skillman, *Biography of a College,* 1:7, 58.

2. Ibid., 37, 54.

3. No doubt because of George Junkin's crucial role in bringing Lafayette to life, he is often mistakenly referred to as the college's founder as well as its first president.

4. Skillman, *Biography of a College,* 1:54, 59.

5. Ibid., 59–61, 65–66.

6. Ibid., 90–91, quotation from 91.

7. Ibid., 117, 62, quotation from 62.

8. Allan, ed., *Life and Letters,* 14, 24.

9. Ibid., 10–11.

10. Ibid., 24. According to Baym, *American Women Writers,* women who wrote tended to write brief lyrics because of the demands of household duties. To some extent, according to Baym, the lyric was seen as "a female form in antebellum America" (68).

11. Allan, ed., *Life and Letters,* 24.

12. See Notebook I and Notebook II.

13. Notebook II, 34. The poem is not dated, but surrounding dated poems indicate that it was written in 1840.

14. Allan, ed., *Life and Letters,* 17.

15. Sketchbook.

16. Coulling, *Margaret Junkin Preston,* 29–30.

17. Sketchbook.

18. Notebook I, 134–35. The poem is not dated, but surrounding dated poems indicate that it was written in January 1840.

19. Notebook II, 94–95.

20. Skillman, *Biography of a College,* 1:60. McCay later became president of the University of South Carolina.

21. Coulling, *Margaret Junkin Preston*, 41.

22. Allan, ed., *Life and Letters*, 21. The letter also appears as "A Letter to Prof. C. F. McC__ of the University of Georgia," in Notebook II, 61–68.

23. Notebook II, 66.

24. Ibid., 94–95.

25. Scrapbook I, 28. The poem was eventually published, but there is no indication as to where.

26. Skillman, *Biography of a College*, 1:130–32. The Porters were an interesting and prominent family. In 1843 James Madison Porter was appointed secretary of war by President John Tyler, but the appointment was never confirmed. See Skillman, 1:15–16.

27. Ibid., 132–33. In his balanced account of Lafayette College's first one hundred years, Skillman maintains that the situation between Porter and Junkin was "really the conflict between two aggressive, determined men, intolerant of any opposition and jealous of their prerogatives" (132).

28. Havighurst, *The Miami Years*, 46, 53–60, 82.

29. Upham, *The Centennial of Miami University*, 330–31.

30. Skillman, *Biography of a College*, 1:103.

31. Ibid., 134.

32. Ibid., 145–46.

33. Ibid., 144–45; Coulling, *Margaret Junkin Preston*, 44–45, quotation from 45. Years later, in 1887, Dr. Charles Elliott, a member of Lafayette's class of 1840, gave a memorial tablet to the college in honor of George Junkin. "The tablet is a token of affection to a man whom I revered and loved, and whose memory I cherish with an undying devotion," Elliott said. "I owe to him more than I do to any other human being." See *Exercises at the Unveiling of the Junkin Memorial Tablet*, quotation from 2.

34. Allan, ed., *Life and Letters*, 16–17, quotation from 16.

35. See Scrapbook I, Scrapbook II, and Scrapbook III.

36. Baym, *American Women Writers*, 68–69.

37. Kelley, *Private Woman, Public Stage*, 126.

38. Scrapbook I, 2. There is no header on this clipping or any other indication of where it was published.

39. Notebook II, 167, 159. Junkin wrote the poem in Notebook II, 167–68, and then had it published. All that is known about Sarah McElroy is that she lived in New York and that her father was a doctor of divinity. The two young women probably became acquainted through their fathers.

40. Several studies in Isenberg and Burstein, eds., *Mortal Remains*, examine the persistence of sentimentality and angelification in antebellum America.

41. Scrapbook I, 2.

42. Ibid.

43. Ibid.

44. Allan, ed., *Life and Letters*, 20. At this point in her life the closest person to Junkin who had died was her brother David, who was born in June 1833 and died nine months later. See Coulling, *Margaret Junkin Preston*, 28.

45. Notebook II, 222–25. The poem also appears on Scrapbook I, 27. It was published in *Neal's Saturday Gazette*, January 18, 1849.

46. Scrapbook I, 27.

47. Notebook II, 121–23, quotation from 121.

48. Douglas, *The Feminization of American Culture,* 6–7, 13.

49. Nye, *The Cultural Life of the New Nation,* 248, 8.

50. Junkin [M.J.], "The Fate of a Rain-Drop," 767.

51. Nye, *The Cultural Life of the New Nation,* 292, 294.

52. Nye, *Society and Culture in America,* 10–12.

53. Baym, *American Women Writers,* 69.

54. Scrapbook I, 2. There is no date or publishing information on this clipping, but it appears in Junkin's scrapbook between "The Early Lost" of March 1841 and "The Fate of a Rain-Drop" of December 1842.

55. Allan, ed., *Life and Letters,* 28.

56. Heron, "George Junkin, D. D., L. L. D.," 97.

57. Havighurst, *The Miami Years,* 83–84. The title of Dr. Junkin's inaugural address was "Obedience to Authority." At one point during the address he proclaimed, "Every good school is a monarchy" (83).

58. Upham, *Centennial of Miami University,* 331.

59. Kraditor, *Means and Ends in American Abolitionism,* 6, 4–5.

60. Potter, *The Impending Crisis,* 40.

61. George Junkin, "*The Integrity of Our National Union,*" 3, 16, 43, 45, 53.

62. Maddex, "Proslavery Millennialism," 475.

63. George Junkin, "*The Integrity of Our National Union,*" 43.

64. Ibid., 78–79, quotation from 79.

65. Ibid., 78.

66. Calhoun to George Junkin, September 17, 1846, in Wilson and Cook, eds., *The Papers of John C. Calhoun,* 23:450–51, quotation from 450.

67. Heron, "George Junkin," 98.

68. Skillman, *Biography of a College,* 1:153.

69. Ibid., 152–53, 157, 158–59, quotation from 157.

70. Ibid., 159.

71. Coulling, *Margaret Junkin Preston,* 48–49, 44.

72. Allan, ed., *Life and Letters,* 23, 22, quotation from 23.

73. Coulling, *Margaret Junkin Preston,* 52.

74. See, for example, Scrapbook I, 27, and Notebook II, 222–25, "A Lament at the Bier of a Student," written while Junkin was in Ohio and published in 1849.

75. Scrapbook I, 27–28, quotation from 27. There is no indication as to where the poem was published.

76. Ibid., 28.

77. Ibid.

78. Baym, *American Women Writers,* 69; May, *The American Female Poets,* 528–29. See also Thomas Buchanan Read, *The Female Poets of America,* 328–32.

79. May, *American Female Poets,* vi, 528–29, quotation from vi.

80. Skillman, *Biography of a College,* 1:173–74, 184–85. According to Skillman, Junkin's "final act" was to file a lawsuit against the college for money he believed was owed him (186).

Chapter 3—"An Intruder in the Field of Literary Labor"

1. O'Brien, *Conjectures of Order,* 264, 266.

2. Fox-Genovese, *Within the Plantation Household,* 247. Caroline Gilman was actively publishing, but Augusta Evans, Caroline Hentz, and Louisa McCord all achieved their greatest fame in the 1850s.

3. Robertson, *Stonewall Jackson,* 131, 127–28. The town of Lexington's population totaled 1,105 whites and 638 blacks in 1850 (see 128). The county's freedmen figure is not surprising. In 1782 the Virginia legislature approved an act stating that emancipation was "judged expedient under certain restrictions." Manumissions in Virginia averaged more than one thousand per year for the next ten years. See Ballagh, *A History of Slavery in Virginia,* 120–21, quotation from 120.

4. Allan, ed., *Life and Letters,* 44–45.

5. Coulling, *Margaret Junkin Preston,* 55, 58.

6. Allan, ed., *Life and Letters,* 45.

7. Ibid., 48–49, quotation from 48. A revision of "The Hallowed Name" was later published in the March 1851 issue of the *Southern Literary Messenger.*

8. Ibid., 48.

9. Ibid., 49.

10. Allan, ed., *Life and Letters,* 46–47, quotation from 47.

11. Ibid., 47, 46.

12. Coulling, *Margaret Junkin Preston,* 58, 63; Crenshaw, *General Lee's College,* 4, 94–95.

13. Allan, ed., *Life and Letters,* 40.

14. Ibid., 49.

15. Ibid., 40.

16. Ibid., 50. Nathaniel Hawthorne's *The Blithedale Romance* was first published in 1852. In mentioning the work Junkin could not help but critique it as well: "Don't you think the newspaper critics are a little too lenient in their judgment of the 'Blithedale Romance' when they say that there is no falling off in it as compared with Hawthorne's other works?" she asked. "To me it seemed quite below 'The House of Seven Gables' in point of interest, of conception, and of artistic finish" (see 50–51).

17. Junkin, "The Reconcilement of the Real and the Ideal," 55–62, quotations from 55.

18. Ibid., 58, 62.

19. Junkin, "Julia," 28–34, quotation from 32.

20. Junkin, "The Death-bed of William the Conqueror," 217; Junkin [M.J.], "The Captive Troubadour," 97–105.

21. Junkin [M.J.], "Hither bring thy Magic Pencil," 272; Junkin, "Autumn," 658–59.

22. Junkin, "An Apostrophe to Niagara," 472.

23. McKinsey, *Niagara Falls,* 3, 2, 37–38, 43.

24. Junkin, "An Apostrophe to Niagara," 472.

25. McKinsey, *Niagara Falls,* 43.

26. Junkin, "An Apostrophe to Niagara," 472.

27. Spencer, *Louis Kossuth and Young America,* 14–15, 22–23.

28. Ibid., 23, 27, 2.

29. Junkin, "Kossuth," 336.

30. Junkin [M.J.], "The Old Dominion: A Ballad," 235–36, quotation from 235.

31. Ibid., 236.

32. Staudenraus, *The African Colonization Movement*, 179, 220, 184, 244.

33. Circular for rally preserved in Notebook II. The poem was later published in an unknown source, with only minor changes, and appears in Scrapbook I, 31. Only a few months later, in "Kossuth," Junkin proclaimed that America was the refuge for all who were fleeing oppression. This seeming paradox was not problematic to Junkin. As her later writings reveal, she, like many of her contemporaries, believed in the innate superiority of the white race.

34. Crenshaw, *General Lee's College*, 115.

35. Johannsen, ed., *Democracy on Trial*, 28–29.

36. Allan, ed., *Life and Letters*, 41–43, quotation from 42–43. See Coulling, *Margaret Junkin Preston*, 81, for information on the publication of these articles. (Copies of Easton newspapers for this time period are no longer available.)

37. Allan, ed., *Life and Letters*, 49–57. Allan misdated the letter November 25, 1850. (See Coulling, *Margaret Junkin Preston*, 81.)

38. Johannsen, ed., *Democracy on Trial*, 29.

39. Allan, ed., *Life and Letters*, 49–57, quotations from 54, 52, and 56–57.

40. Ibid., 54, 55, 57.

41. Junkin's attitude is consistent with that described by Fox-Genovese in *Within the Plantation Household*. Junkin did not feel kinship with slave women because of gender; to her, race was a more important factor.

42. Robertson, *Stonewall Jackson*, 144, 115, 44, 69–79, 111, 122, 121.

43. Ibid., 145; Margaret Junkin Preston, "Personal Reminiscences of Stonewall Jackson," 927.

44. Junkin, *Silverwood*, 314, 354–55. Junkin's only novel, *Silverwood*, was highly autobiographical, as she admitted. See also Robertson, *Stonewall Jackson*, 145. Junkin's feelings were probably not the only reason that Eleanor called off the engagement. Historians who have studied nineteenth-century courtship have noted that it was a fairly common practice for women temporarily to break an engagement. Rothman, *Hands and Hearts: A History of Courtship in America*, notes that marriage imposed a "double burden" on a woman (66). She was responsible for the happiness and virtue of her new family while also completely dependent on her husband. It is not surprising that many women were reluctant to leave their birth families for such an arrangement. Lystra, *Searching the Heart: Women, Men, and Romantic Love in Nineteenth-Century America*, adds that these hesitations served as "tests of love" (10). A man who remained devoted proved to a woman that he was worthy of her future dependence on him.

45. Junkin, *Silverwood*, 355–57, quotation from 356.

46. Ibid., 357.

47. Robertson, *Stonewall Jackson*, 147.

48. Preston, "Personal Reminiscences of Stonewall Jackson," 927, 930–32, quotation from 932. Wedding trips (not yet called honeymoons) were common by 1840, and couples were frequently accompanied by relatives and close friends. Niagara Falls was a popular destination. See Rothman, *Hands and Hearts*, 82.

49. Coulling, *Margaret Junkin Preston*, 71–72.

50. Robertson, *Stonewall Jackson,* 144, 153; Junkin, *Silverwood,* 379–81.

51. Junkin, *Silverwood,* 381–82. Julia was fifteen years her junior, and Junkin probably did not believe that theirs could be an emotionally intimate relationship. See note 72 for this chapter regarding the relationship between Junkin and her father.

52. Junkin, *Silverwood,* 384–86, quotation from 384–85.

53. Robertson, *Stonewall Jackson,* 157, 160.

54. Ibid., 162.

55. Allan, ed., *Life and Letters,* 73.

56. Ibid., 73–74.

57. Robertson, *Stonewall Jackson,* 163.

58. Allan, ed., *Life and Letters,* 74.

59. Robertson, *Stonewall Jackson,* 163. This letter was written by Jackson on March 1, 1855.

60. Robertson, *Stonewall Jackson,* 164; Preston, "Personal Reminiscences of Stonewall Jackson," 932, quotations from 932.

61. Preston, "Personal Reminiscences of Stonewall Jackson," 927–28, quotations from 928.

62. Robertson believes that Junkin and Jackson were in love by fall 1856. See *Stonewall Jackson,* 174. Coulling speculates about their feelings for one another in *Margaret Junkin Preston,* 85–87. A canon in the Presbyterian Church forbade a man marrying his deceased wife's sister.

63. Scrapbook I, 3–6, quotation from 5.

64. Ibid., 5.

65. Ibid., 6–25.

66. Hubbell, *The South in American Literature,* 603.

67. Moss, *Domestic Novelists in the Old South.*

68. Ibid., 5.

69. Junkin, *Silverwood,* 266–67, quotation from 266.

70. Junkin, *Silverwood;* Coulling, *Margaret Junkin Preston,* 83.

71. Allan, ed., *Life and Letters,* 85.

72. The absence in *Silverwood* of a character representing George Junkin is rather surprising. Throughout all her trials, there is no evidence that Margaret Junkin considered her father a source of comfort. Perhaps his absence in the novel indicates that theirs was a relationship based on intellect, not emotion; or perhaps Junkin was speculating about navigating her own course without her father's strong presence.

73. Junkin, *Silverwood,* 15–16.

74. Ibid., 87, 312, 313.

75. Ibid., 382.

76. Ibid., 174–75.

77. Ibid., 175.

78. Ibid., 174, 176–77.

79. Junkin's rejection of domesticity in *Silverwood* has led Baym, in *Woman's Fiction,* to argue that the novel is "irrelevant to woman's fiction" (241). According to Baym, women writers in the mid-nineteenth century were attempting to better their condition through a "domestic ideology." The values of the home were to be projected onto the

world, thereby eradicating the notion of separate spheres and increasing the status of those individuals who dominated the home: women. An understanding of Junkin's body of work demonstrates that *Silverwood* is relevant, even crucial, to woman's fiction. Junkin was a few steps ahead of many of her contemporaries; she had moved beyond the "domestic ideology" and made several attempts at expanding woman's place. The tone of defeat in *Silverwood* is Junkin's acknowledgment that her arguments had not been successful.

80. Moss, *Domestic Novelists*, 10.

81. Review of *Silverwood*, *Southern Literary Messenger* 24 (January 1857): 80.

82. Coulling, *Margaret Junkin Preston*, 88, 87.

Chapter 4—Family Ties Formed and Severed

1. Bryan, ed., *A March Past*, 87–88.

2. Ibid., xiv, 13, 33; Robertson, *Stonewall Jackson*, 167. John Preston's name appeared on the flyer advertising the December 1849 rally for the immigrants to Liberia.

3. Bryan, ed., *A March Past*, 35, 40, 44, 48, 93.

4. Ibid., 88. 93–94; Robertson, *Stonewall Jackson*, 144; quotation from Bryan, ed., *A March Past*, 88. John Preston was given the honorary rank of major because of his position at the Virginia Military Institute. See Coulling, *Margaret Junkin Preston*, 91–92.

5. Allan, ed., *Life and Letters*, 107.

6. Bryan, ed., *A March Past*, 19, 88, 87, 89–90, quotations from 88, 87, and 89.

7. Ibid., 93–94.

8. Allan, ed., *Life and Letters*, 100.

9. Bryan, ed., *A March Past*, 94–95, quotation from 95.

10. Ibid., 94.

11. Coulling, *Margaret Junkin Preston*, 102, 104, 110; Bryan, ed., *A March Past*, 140, 99.

12. Potter, *The Impending Crisis*, 43.

13. Crenshaw, *General Lee's College*, 116–17; Coulling, *Margaret Junkin Preston*, 107.

14. Allan, ed., *Life and Letters*, 110–11; Robertson, *Stonewall Jackson*, 196–97.

15. John T. L. Preston to Margaret J. Preston, December 2, 1859, published in Allan, ed., *Life and Letters*, 111–17, quotation from 111–12.

16. Ibid., 114–15.

17. Bryan, ed., *A March Past*, 115.

18. George Junkin, *An Address Delivered before the Literary Societies of Rutgers College*.

19. George Junkin, *Political Fallacies*, 12.

20. Bryan, ed., *A March Past*, 115.

21. Robertson, *Stonewall Jackson*, 206–8.

22. Junkin, *Political Fallacies*, 11–12, quotations from 12.

23. Ibid., 12–13, quotation from 13.

24. Robertson, *Stonewall Jackson*, 211.

25. Junkin, *Political Fallacies*, 13–18, quotation from 14. Junkin's entire account of his final days at Washington College appears on 11–18.

26. Ibid., 18.

27. Crenshaw, *General Lee's College*, 124.

28. Robertson, *Stonewall Jackson*, 212, 224; Allan, ed., *Life and Letters*, 117.

29. John T. L. Preston to Margaret J. Preston, [Spring 1861], published in Allan, ed., *Life and Letters,* quotations from 117; John T. L. Preston to Margaret J. Preston, May 12, 1861, published in ibid., 118.

30. Preston [M.J.P.], "Elizabeth Barrett Browning," 146–53.

31. Ibid., 146.

32. Ibid., 149.

33. Ibid.

34. Ibid., 148.

35. Ibid., 146.

36. Ibid., 148, 146–47, quotation from 147.

Chapter 5—Wielding the Pen

1. John T. L. Preston to Margaret J. Preston, December 23, 1861, published in Allan, ed., *Life and Letters,* 126–27, quotation from 126.

2. Historians have noted this increase in women's writing, but they have often failed to recognize its significance. See Rable, *Civil Wars,* and Faust, *Mothers of Invention.* Both Rable and Faust have concluded that any changes the war brought were not welcomed by Southern women. Assuming that women authors largely viewed their writing endeavors as necessary evils, Rable and Faust do not fully acknowledge the level of success attained by some women and the positive impact this development had on their lives and the lives of other women.

3. This chapter does not intend to enter into the debate regarding the strength, or existence, of Confederate nationalism. Those who doubt its existence acknowledge that there was a "pretend nationalism." Whether Preston served a "pretend" Confederate nationalism or a real one, she nevertheless served a nationalism. Quotation from Beringer, Hattaway, Jones, and Still, *Why the South Lost the Civil War,* 81.

4. See Jones, *Tomorrow Is Another Day,* and Fahs, *The Imagined Civil War.*

5. Allan, ed., *Life and Letters,* 143.

6. Coulling, *Margaret Junkin Preston,* 235; Simms, ed., *War Poetry of the South,* 433–36.

7. Simms, ed., *War Poetry of the South,* 435.

8. Ibid., 435–36.

9. Clinton, *Tara Revisited,* observes other ways in which Confederate nationalism allowed women to expand their place. Clinton notes women who acted as nurses, spies, smugglers, and soldiers, as well as women who performed in government jobs.

10. Allan, ed., *Life and Letters,* 134 and 143–44.

11. Ibid., 137–39, quotation from 137.

12. Ibid., 140–42.

13. Ibid., 147–48, quotations from 147–48; Coulling, *Margaret Junkin Preston,* 99, 126.

14. Allan, ed., *Life and Letters,* 148–49, quotation from 149.

15. Preston, *Beechenbrook,* 61–63, quotation from 61.

16. Allan, ed., *Life and Letters,* 156–58, quotation from 157–58.

17. Scrapbook II, 148.

18. Allan, ed., *Life and Letters,* 158–59.

19. Ibid., 156.

20. George Junkin, *Political Fallacies.*

21. Allan, ed., *Life and Letters,* 157.

22. Ibid., 142–43, 145, 163–65.

23. Ibid., 165.

24. Preston, *Cartoons,* 182–83.

25. Coulling, *Margaret Junkin Preston,* 139–40.

26. Preston, *Cartoons,* 183.

27. Allan, ed., *Life and Letters,* 167.

28. Ibid.

29. Blair, *Virginia's Private War,* argues that the Union army created a Virginia-Confederate identity by providing evidence of a barbaric enemy. Northern actions against civilians increasingly convinced Virginians that Yankees were different.

30. Allan, ed., *Life and Letters,* quotations from 180; Coulling, *Margaret Junkin Preston,* 136.

31. Brice, *Conquest of a Valley,* vi; Eby, ed., *A Virginia Yankee in the Civil War,* 234.

32. Grimsley, *The Hard Hand of War,* 2–3; Ash, *When the Yankees Came,* 50–56; Phillips, *The Shenandoah Valley in 1864,* 1–9.

33. Phillips, *The Shenandoah Valley in 1864,* 7. For comments about General Hunter see, for example, Beach, *The First New York (Lincoln) Cavalry,* 371; Du Pont, *The Campaign of 1864,* 37, 68–69; Williams, ed., *Diary and Letters of Rutherford Birchard Hayes,* 473–74, 478–79.

34. Allan, ed., *Life and Letters,* 189.

35. Ibid., 189–91.

36. Ibid., 190–91.

37. Ibid., 193.

38. *War Lyrics and Songs of the South,* 2.

39. Allan, ed., *Life and Letters,* 192.

40. Du Pont, *The Campaign of 1864,* 70; Allan, ed., *Life and Letters,* 196–97; quotation from 196.

41. Bryan, ed., *A March Past,* 166.

42. Allan, ed., *Life and Letters,* 197.

43. Scrapbook II, 113; Coulling, *Margaret Junkin Preston,* 235; Simms, ed., *War Poetry of the South,* 55.

44. Scrapbook II, 115; Coulling, *Margaret Junkin Preston,* 235.

45. Preston's experience during the war years is opposite the experience described by Faust in *Mothers of Invention;* Faust has maintained that elite Southern women increasingly placed personal needs ahead of national needs. According to Faust, the more losses women endured, the more they withdrew their support of the Confederacy. Though she used Preston as an example of a woman whose support of the Confederacy eroded, Faust quoted a diary entry from September 1862 (recounted in this chapter). Yet, Preston's attitude changed dramatically after 1862. See Faust, *Mothers of Invention,* 238.

46. Preston, *Beechenbrook.*

47. Allan, ed., *Life and Letters,* 199, 203.

48. See Gardner, *Blood and Irony,* quotation from 31.

49. Allan, ed., 172, 177, 203; Bryan, ed., *A March Past,* 182.

50. Preston, *Beechenbrook,* 7.
51. Ibid., 12.
52. See Gardner, *Blood and Irony.*
53. Preston, *Beechenbrook,* 7.
54. Ibid., 51.
55. Ibid., 64.
56. Allan, ed., *Life and Letters,* 202–3.
57. Ibid., 207–8.

Chapter 6—Conquering by "Force of Thought"

1. Allan, ed., *Life and Letters,* 210.
2. Coulling, *Margaret Junkin Preston,* 148.
3. Allan, ed., *Life and Letters,* 208. Allan chose not to publish many of Preston's entries after the war, saying, "The story of reconstruction has no place here." The whereabouts of these entries is not known (see 208).
4. Coulling, *Margaret Junkin Preston,* 148–49.
5. Allan, ed., *Life and Letters,* 211–12.
6. Foster, *Ghosts of the Confederacy,* 36–37.
7. Preston, *Beechenbrook* (1866), 3.
8. Hubbell, *The South in American Literature,* 712, 710.
9. Preston, *Beechenbrook* (1866); Foster, *Ghosts of the Confederacy,* 36.
10. Preston, *Beechenbrook* (1866), 92–94.
11. Allan, ed., *Life and Letters,* 241–42, quotation from 242.
12. Hubbell, *The South in American Literature,* 523; *Southern Field and Fireside* review, republished in Tardy, ed., *The Living Female Writers of the South,* 382, 384.
13. Tardy, ed., *The Living Female Writers of the South,* 380–82; Hubbell, *The South in American Literature,* 726, 761.
14. *Round Table* review, republished in Tardy, ed., *The Living Female Writers of the South,* 380.
15. Ibid., 382.
16. *Southern Field and Fireside* review, republished in Tardy, ed., *The Living Female Writers of the South,* 385.
17. Coulling, *Margaret Junkin Preston,* 152; Allan, ed., *Life and Letters,* 241–42.
18. Davidson, *The Living Writers of the South,* 431–38, quotations from 431 and 434; Hubbell, *The South in American Literature,* 524.
19. Davidson, *The Living Writers of the South,* 432, 434–38, quotation from 432.
20. Lowe, "Another Look at Reconstruction in Virginia," 56–76; see also 63–64, 67, 69.
21. Scrapbook III, 4. The poem was published, but it is unclear when or where.
22. Lowe, "Another Look at Reconstruction in Virginia," 69.
23. Ibid., 70, 75–76, 57.
24. Preston, "General Lee after the War," 271–72, quotation from 271.
25. Ibid., 271–72.
26. Ibid., 273.
27. Ibid.
28. Allan, ed., *Life and Letters,* 221.

29. Ibid., 218.

30. Preston, "General Lee after the War," 275–76.

31. Allan, ed., *Life and Letters*, 237–39, 258–59, quotations from 238 and 258.

32. Preston, *Cartoons*, 180–81, quotation from 180.

33. Allan, ed., *Life and Letters*, 222–24. The "Pass" refers to the Goshen Pass, part of the route from Lexington to Richmond. There remains no explicit explanation as to why Preston could not attend the service.

34. Preston, *Cartoons*, 189–91, quotation from 189.

35. Hayne to Preston, December 31, 1867, published in Allan, ed., *Life and Letters*, 243.

36. Moore, ed., *A Man of Letters in the Nineteenth-Century South*, 12.

37. Hubbell, *The South in American Literature*, 744–50.

38. Ibid., 710.

39. Hayne to Preston, December 31, 1867, published in Allan, ed., *Life and Letters*, 243.

40. Preston to Hayne, February 14, 1868, published in Allan, ed., *Life and Letters*, 244–45, quotation from 244.

41. Ibid.

42. Ibid., 245.

43. Preston to Hayne, July 11, 1869, published in Allan, ed., *Life and Letters*, 245–47, quotation from 246.

44. Allan, ed., *Life and Letters*, 226–29.

45. Preston to Hayne, July 11, 1869, published in Allan, ed., *Life and Letters*, 246.

46. Hayne to Preston, August 29, 1871, published in Moore, ed., *A Man of Letters in the Nineteenth-Century South*, 84–88, quotation from 85–86.

47. Hayne to Preston, April 9, 1872, published in Moore, ed., *A Man of Letters in the Nineteenth-Century South*, 96–101, quotations from 100.

48. Preston to Hayne, September 13, 1869, published in Allan, ed., *Life and Letters*, 249–55, quotation from 249.

49. Hubbell, *The South in American Literature*, 717.

50. Preston to Hayne, September 13, 1869, published in Allan, ed., *Life and Letters*, 249–50.

51. Moore, "'Courtesies of the Guild' and More," 491.

52. Allan, ed., *Life and Letters*, 258. Preston's concern about Southern journals was well placed. After the war many literary and semiliterary magazines were founded in hopes of serving as bastions of Southern intellectual thought and development. One by one, they failed. Part of the problem was the lack of a stable publishing house in the South, and the fact that most of the editors were new to the business. Editors and publishers did not know how to market their products and could pay their contributors very little, if anything. Many educated Southerners could not afford magazine subscriptions in the years after the war, and those who could often preferred Northern or British magazines. In 1867 the *Atlantic Monthly* boasted a circulation of approximately fifty or sixty thousand, while *Land We Love*, one of the more successful Southern journals, edited by General Daniel H. Hill, claimed twelve thousand, many of those nonpaying. *Land We Love* was absorbed by the *New Eclectic* in April 1869. The *New Eclectic*, renamed the *Southern Magazine*, lasted until December 1875. See Hubbell, *The South in American Literature*, 716–20.

53. Preston to Hayne, September 13, 1869, published in Allan, ed., *Life and Letters,* 254.

54. Allan, ed., *Life and Letters,* 230–33, quotations from 231 and 233.

55. Ibid., 236.

56. Ibid.

57. Preston, *Old Song and New;* Hubbell, *The South in American Literature,* 726–27, 766.

58. Preston, *Old Song and New,* 5.

59. Ibid., 85–89, quotation from 86–87.

60. Ibid., 191–96, quotation from 196.

61. Preston to Hayne, September 9, 1870, published in Allan, ed., *Life and Letters,* 255–57, quotations from 255 and 256.

62. John T. L. Preston to Hayne, October 8, 1870, published in Allan, ed., *Life and Letters,* 257–58. Hayne did eventually write a review of *Old Song and New,* but it remains unclear where it was published. On May 27, 1871, Preston wrote Hayne to thank him for his "most flattering and charming and elaborate criticism." "*Old Song and New* has never been so honored by any extended notice," she continued, "and I offer you my hearty thanks for this gentle labor of love." See Allan, ed., *Life and Letters,* 259–60.

63. *Saturday Review* critique, republished in Tardy, ed., *Living Female Writers,* 379–80.

64. Preston did have one complaint about the review, writing in her diary: "It says I wrote 'Greek Stories' after reading Lowell's 'Rhoecus' and 'Tales of Miletus.' I have never known until tonight that Lowell wrote 'Rhoecus,' and I wrote 'The Flight of the Arethusa' before I ever heard of Lord Lytton's book." See Allan, ed., *Life and Letters,* 241.

65. Hayne to Preston, April 9, 1872, published in Moore, ed., *A Man of Letters in the Nineteenth-Century South,* 96.

Chapter 7—"I Think I May Sing"

1. Allan, ed., *Life and Letters,* 266–68.

2. Preston's additional appearances in *Lippincott's* during the 1870s were "Nocturne" (August 1878) and "Not Worth the While" (February 1879). Hubbell, *The South in American Literature,* 727.

3. Thompson to Preston, June 20, 1872, published in Allan, ed., *Life and Letters,* 264–66, quotations from 265.

4. Preston to Hayne, September 13, 1869, published in Allan, ed., *Life and Letters,* 250.

5. Allan, ed., *Life and Letters,* quotations from 270; Hubbell, *The South in American Literature,* 524. John R. Thompson may have had a hand in Preston's appearance in the *Albion.* He used to work at that journal, and Preston stated in her diary that he sent her ten copies of the issue of *Albion* that included her poem.

6. Preston, *Cartoons,* 186.

7. Ibid.

8. Ibid., 187–88, quotation from 188.

9. Allan, ed., *Life and Letters,* 271–72, quotation from 272.

10. Coulling, *Margaret Junkin Preston,* 176.

11. Allan, ed., *Life and Letters,* 272.

12. Hayne to Preston, April 9, 1872, published in Moore, ed., *A Man of Letters in the Nineteenth-Century South,* 96 and 97.

13. Ibid., 96.

14. Moore, ed., *A Man of Letters in the Nineteenth-Century South*, 102.

15. Ibid., 117, 119, quotation from 119.

16. Ibid., 117, 121, 118, quotation from 118.

17. Hayne to Preston, May 12, 1874, published in Moore, ed., *A Man of Letters in the Nineteenth-Century South*, 117–20, quotation from 117–18.

18. Ibid., 120.

19. Hubbell, *The South in American Literature*, 754.

20. Ibid.

21. Moore, "Introduction to Part II," in *The History of Southern Literature*, 177; Skaggs, "Varieties of Local Color," in *The History of Southern Literature*, 224; Moore, "Poetry of the Late Nineteenth Century," in *The History of Southern Literature*, 193, 195.

22. Hayne to Preston, May 12, 1874, published in Moore, ed., *A Man of Letters in the Nineteenth-Century South*, 118, 120.

23. Preston, *Cartoons*.

24. Ibid., 7–10, quotation from 7.

25. Ibid., 8–10.

26. Ibid., 70–72.

27. Ibid., 70–71.

28. Ibid., 71.

29. Ibid., 210–13, quotations from 212 and 213.

30. Ibid., 213.

31. Preston, "Nocturne," 196.

32. Coulling, *Margaret Junkin Preston*, 163; Allan, ed., *Life and Letters*, 303–4. Quotation from Allan, ed., 304.

33. Coulling, *Margaret Junkin Preston*, 164, 163, 165–66.

34. Preston to Allan, 1876, published in Allan, ed., *Life and Letters*, 293–94, quotation from 293.

35. Scrapbook III, 26.

36. Preston to Allan, 1877, published in Allan, ed., *Life and Letters*, 291.

37. Allan, ed., *Life and Letters*, 289.

38. Ibid., 290.

39. Coulling, *Margaret Junkin Preston*, 168; Review of *Cartoons*, *Lippincott's* 17 (May 1876): 647.

40. Hayne, *The Mountain of the Lovers*, 3.

41. Allan, ed., *Life and Letters*, 274–75; Moore, ed., *A Man of Letters in the Nineteenth-Century South*, 160.

42. Whittier to Preston, November 27, 1875, published in Allan, ed., *Life and Letters*, 275; Whittier, ed., *Songs of Three Centuries*, 321. *Songs of Three Centuries* contains the works of 307 English-speaking poets active from the mid-sixteenth century to the 1870s. Hayne also appeared in the volume.

43. Longfellow to Preston, November 23, 1875, published in Allan, ed., *Life and Letters*, 274.

44. Arvin, *Longfellow*, 133.

45. Longfellow to Preston, November 23, 1875, published in Allan, ed., *Life and Letters,* 274. *Poems of Places* was published in thirty-one volumes between 1876 and 1879. Longfellow eventually used five of Preston's poems: "The Lady Riberta's Harvest" (15:267–71) from *Cartoons;* "Bacharach Wine" (18:159–61) also from *Cartoons;* "A Bit of Autumn Color" (28:44); "A November Nocturne" (28:206–7); and "Maximilian at Queretaro" (30:153–55), which appeared in *Old Song and New* as "Poor Carlotta" (164–66).

46. Folders 101/4 and 101/5, Special Collections, Leyburn Library, Washington and Lee University.

47. Allan, ed., *Life and Letters,* 240, 290.

48. Moore, ed., *A Man of Letters in the Nineteenth-Century South,* 97, 102.

49. Allan, ed., *Life and Letters,* 240.

50. Hayne to Preston, December 15, 1871, published in Moore, ed., *A Man of Letters in the Nineteenth-Century South,* 91–94, quotation from 93.

51. Hubbell, *The South in American Literature,* 756.

52. Preston to Hayne, December 26, 1877, published in Allan, ed., *Life and Letters,* 296–99, quotation from 298.

53. Allan, ed., *Life and Letters,* 291–92; Preston to Allan, May 5, 1877, published in Allan, ed., *Life and Letters,* quotation from 290.

54. Scott, *Natural Allies,* 85–86, 2.

55. Allan, ed., *Life and Letters,* 292.

Chapter 8—"My Work Is Done"

1. Hayne to Preston, January 8, 1881, published in Moore, ed., *A Man of Letters in the Nineteenth-Century South,* 167–69, quotation from 168.

2. Preston to Hayne, December 1, 1881, published in Allan, ed., *Life and Letters,* 301–2.

3. Preston to Hayne, December 26, 1877, published in Allan, ed., *Life and Letters,* 296–99, quotation from 299.

4. Allan, ed., *Life and Letters,* 300–1, quotation from 301.

5. Preston, "An Acorn's Lesson," 288. Preston's other appearances in *Lippincott's* during the first half of the 1880s include "Persephone" (May 1880), "The Wanderer's Bell" (January 1881), and "The American Sculptor Ezekiel" (June 1883).

6. Scrapbook III, 1–3, quotations from 1 and 3.

7. Preston to S.G. [Sophia Gilman], September 9, 1883, published in Allan, ed., *Life and Letters,* 317–19, quotation from 318; Coulling, *Margaret Junkin Preston,* 246.

8. Preston to S.G., September 9, 1883, published in Allan, ed., *Life and Letters,* 317–19, quotation from 318.

9. Ibid.

10. Ibid., 317.

11. Hayne to Preston, October 9, 1882, published in Moore, ed., *A Man of Letters in the Nineteenth-Century South,* 202–5; Hayne to Preston, April 11, 1882, published in ibid., 190–92, quotation from 190.

12. Preston to S.G., September 9, 1883, published in Allan, ed., *Life and Letters,* 318 and 318–19.

13. Allan, ed., *Life and Letters,* 303.

14. Scrapbook III, 99. It is unclear where the poem was published.

15. Allan, ed., *Life and Letters*, 307–8, 295.

16. Ibid., 307–12, quotation from 307; Coulling, *Margaret Junkin Preston*, 181.

17. Moore, ed., *A Man of Letters in the Nineteenth-Century South*, 218.

18. Allan, ed., *Life and Letters*, 308; Preston to Hayne, June 28, 1884, and August 20, 1884, published in Allan, ed., *Life and Letters*, 308–12, quotations from 310 and 311.

19. Preston to Hayne, June 28, 1884, and August 20, 1884, in Allan, ed., *Life and Letters*, 308–12, quotations from 310, 308, and 311.

20. Preston to Hayne, June 28, 1884, in Allan, ed., *Life and Letters*, 308–10.

21. Preston, *A Handful of Monographs*, 219.

22. Preston to Hayne, October 20, 1884, published in Allan, ed., *Life and Letters*, 312–13, quotations from 312.

23. Allan, ed., *Life and Letters*, 317.

24. Coulling, *Margaret Junkin Preston*, 183.

25. Allan, ed., *Life and Letters*, 369.

26. Preston, *A Handful of Monographs*.

27. G. J. Preston, "Alpenglow," 606–7.

28. Preston, *Centennial Poem: 1775–1885*, 24. At the time the university did not recognize the founding of Liberty Hall Academy in 1749 as the beginning of its history. See Coulling, *Margaret Junkin Preston*, 190. There is no evidence as to why the celebration was held ten years late.

29. Hayne to Preston, October 11, 1885, published in Moore, ed., *A Man of Letters in the Nineteenth-Century South*, 283–85, quotations from 284–85 and 284.

30. Preston to S.G., May 15, 1886, published in Allan, ed., *Life and Letters*, 319–21, quotation from 320.

31. Preston, *For Love's Sake*.

32. See Cox, *Dixie's Daughters*.

33. Rable, *Civil Wars*, and Faust, *Mothers of Invention*, argue that Southern white women's contributions to the Lost Cause can be seen as evidence that these women were embracing the traditional patriarchy of the South. Cox, *Dixie's Daughters*, argues that women were leaders of the Lost Cause movement, and through it they shaped the social and political culture of the New South. Preston's life and career demonstrate that women used the movement as a vehicle through which to perform in nontraditional ways.

34. Preston, "Personal Reminiscences of Stonewall Jackson," 927.

35. Preston, "General Lee after the War," 271.

36. Preston, *Colonial Ballads*.

37. Preston to Mrs. Paul H. Hayne, June 24, 1886, published in Allan, ed., *Life and Letters*, 314–16, quotation from 316.

38. Hubbell, *The South in American Literature*, 755.

39. Hayne to Preston, January 6, 1886, published in Moore, ed., *A Man of Letters in the Nineteenth-Century South*, 299–302; Charles Egbert Craddock [Mary N. Murfree], *In the Tennessee Mountains*.

40. Preston, "Aunt Dorothy's Funeral."

41. Mackethan, "Plantation Fiction, 1865–1900," in *The History of Southern Literature*, 210–11.

42. Preston, "Aunt Dorothy's Funeral."

43. Coulling, *Margaret Junkin Preston,* 198; Moore, "Introduction to Part II," 177.

44. Withrow Scrapbooks 19: 107, Special Collections, Leyburn Library, Washington and Lee University.

45. Ibid.

46. Allan, ed., *Life and Letters,* 321–23, quotation from 321.

47. Coulling, *Margaret Junkin Preston,* 188.

48. Preston to S.G., January 13, 1891, published in Allan, ed., *Life and Letters,* 323–24, quotations from 323. Coulling refers to the "nervous illness" as a stroke; see *Margaret Junkin Preston,* 188.

49. Allan, ed., *Life and Letters,* 325.

50. Preston to General G. W. C. Lee, May 11, 1891, Special Collections, Leyburn Library, Washington and Lee University.

51. Preston, "Giving Children Right Impressions of Death," 707–8.

52. Allan, ed., *Life and Letters,* 326; Margaret J. Preston to A. De F., no date given, published in Allan, ed., *Life and Letters,* 327–29, quotation from 327.

53. Allan, ed., *Life and Letters,* 326–27; Coulling, *Margaret Junkin Preston,* 197.

54. Buchanan to Miss G. [Sophia Gilman], March 27, 1897, published in Allan, ed., *Life and Letters,* 335–36, quotation from 336.

55. Allan, ed., *Life and Letters,* 336, 337–38.

Conclusion

1. Coulling, *Margaret Junkin Preston,* 156.

SELECT BIBLIOGRAPHY

Manuscripts

Duke University, William R. Perkins Library
    Paul Hamilton Hayne Papers
University of North Carolina, Southern Historical Collection
    Thomas Jonathan Jackson Papers
    Margaret Junkin Preston Papers
Washington and Lee University, Leyburn Library, Special Collections
    Margaret Junkin Preston Papers
    Rockbridge Historical Society Collection
    Withrow Scrapbooks

Selected Works of Margaret Junkin Preston

In chronological order

"Lines Addressed to Sister Eleanor." Unpublished, [1840]. Notebook I, 134–35.

"Hawthorn Bower." Unpublished, [1840]. Notebook II, 34.

"A Letter to Prof. C. F. McC__ of the University of Georgia." Unpublished, November 13, 1840. Notebook II, 61–68.

"To _____ _____." [Circa 1840]. Scrapbook I, 28.

"To _____ ." Unpublished, February 1841. Notebook II, 94–95.

"The Early Lost." [March 17, 1841]. Scrapbook I, 2.

"When a Few Years Are Come, Then I Shall Go the Way Whence I Shall Not Return." Unpublished, July 1841. Notebook II, 121–23.

"Song." [1842]. Scrapbook I, 2.

"The Fate of a Rain-Drop." *Southern Literary Messenger* 8 (December 1842): 767.

"A Ballad in Reply to Martin Farquhar Tupper's 'New Ballad to Columbia.'" [Circa 1848]. Scrapbook I, 27–28.

"Galileo before the Inquisition." In *The American Female Poets: With Biographical and Critical Notices,* by Caroline May, 528–29. Philadelphia: Lindsay & Blakiston, 1848.

"A Lament at the Bier of a Student." January 18, 1849. Scrapbook I, 27.

"The Old Dominion: A Ballad." *Southern Literary Messenger* 15 (April 1849): 235–36.

"An Apostrophe to Niagara." *Southern Literary Messenger* 15 (August 1849): 472.

"Stanzas." [1849]. Scrapbook I, 31.

"Hither Bring Thy Magic Pencil." *Southern Literary Messenger* 16 (May 1850): 272.

"Kossuth." *Sartain's* 6 (May 1850): 336.

"The Hallowed Name." *Southern Literary Messenger* 17 (March 1851): 147.

"Julia: A Sketch of Ancient Rome." *Sartain's* 9 (July 1851): 28–34.

"Autumn." *Southern Literary Messenger* 17 (October-November 1851): 658–59.

"The Reconcilement of the Real and the Ideal." *Sartain's* 10 (January 1852): 55–62.

"The Death-bed of William the Conqueror: An Historic Ballad." *Southern Literary Messenger* 18 (April 1852): 217.

"The Captive Troubadour: An Historical Sketch of the Olden Time." *Southern Literary Messenger* 19 (February 1853): 97–105.

"The Child of Song." [1855]. Scrapbook I, 3–6.

"The Virginia Colonist; A Story of Early Times." [1855]. Scrapbook I, 6–12.

"The Ashburnes; A Tale of Seventy-Seven." [1855]. Scrapbook I, 12–25.

Silverwood: Book of Memories. New York: Derby & Jackson, 1856.

"Elizabeth Barrett Browning." *Southern Literary Messenger* 30 (February 1860): 146–53.

"Dirge for Ashby." [1862]. In *War Poetry of the South*, edited by William Gilmore Simms, 433–36. New York: Richardson, 1867.

"Christmas Carol, for 1862." [1862]. Scrapbook II, 148.

"Stonewall Jackson's Grave." [1864]. In *War Lyrics and Songs of the South*, 1–4. London: Spottiswoode, 1866.

"Hymn to the National Flag." November 2, 1864. Scrapbook II, 113. Republished in *War Poetry of the South*, 55–57.

"A Christmas Lay for 1864: When the War Is Over." January 4, 1865. Scrapbook II, 115.

Beechenbrook: A Rhyme of the War. Richmond: J. W. Randolph, 1865; revised and enlarged edition, Baltimore: Kelly & Piet, 1866.

"Virginia's Reply to the Vote of October, 1867." [1867]. Scrapbook III, 4.

Old Song and New. Philadelphia: Lippincott, 1870.

"Vittoria Colonna to Michael Angelo." *Lippincott's* 7 (May 1871): 492–94.

A May Night Masque. May 1872. Folders 101/4 and 101/5, Special Collections, Leyburn Library, Washington and Lee University.

"Mona Lisa's Picture." *Lippincott's* 10 (July 1872): 27–28.

"Andrea's Mistake." *Lippincott's* 10 (September 1872): 277–78.

Cartoons. Boston: Roberts, 1875.

"Tintoretto's Last Picture." *Lippincott's* 16 (October 1875): 413–14.

"The Lady Riberta's Harvest." In *Poems of Places*, edited by Henry Wadsworth Longfellow, 15:267–71. 31 vols. Boston: Osgood, 1876–79.

"Bacharach Wine." In *Poems of Places*, 18:159–61.

"A Bit of Autumn Color." In *Poems of Places*, 28:44.

"A November Nocturne." 28: 206–7

"Maximilian at Queretaro." In *Poems of Places*, 30:153–55.

"Nocturne." *Lippincott's* 22 (August 1878): 196.

"Not Worth the While." *Lippincott's* 23 (February 1879): 247.

"Persephone." *Lippincott's* 25 (May 1880): 611–12.

"The Literary Profession in the South." 1881. Scrapbook III, 1–3.

"The Wanderer's Bell." *Lippincott's* 27 (January 1881): 41–42.

"An Acorn's Lesson." *Lippincott's* 28 (September 1881): 288.

"Georgie's and Herbert's Letter." [Circa 1881]. Scrapbook III, 26.

"Winter Love. A Wife's Letter." [Circa 1882]. Scrapbook III, 99.

"The American Sculptor Ezekiel." *Lippincott's* 31 (June 1883): 620–23.

Centennial Poem: 1775–1885. New York: Putnam, 1885.

A Handful of Monographs: Continental and English. New York: A. D. F. Randolph, 1886.

For Love's Sake: Poems of Faith and Comfort. New York: A. D. F. Randolph, 1886.

"Personal Reminiscences of Stonewall Jackson." *Century Illustrated Monthly Magazine* 10 (October 1886): 927–36.

Colonial Ballads, Sonnets and Other Verse. Boston: Houghton, Mifflin, 1887.

"General Lee after the War." *Century Illustrated Monthly Magazine* 16 (June 1889): 271–76.

"Aunt Dorothy's Funeral." *Harper's New Monthly Magazine* 79 (October 1889): 745–60.

"Giving Children Right Impressions of Death." *Sunday School Times* 33 (November 7, 1891): 707–8.

Additional Primary Sources

Allan, Elizabeth Preston, ed. *The Life and Letters of Margaret Junkin Preston.* Boston: Houghton, Mifflin, 1903.

Beach, William H. *The First New York (Lincoln) Cavalry, from April 19, 1861 to July 7, 1865.* New York: Lincoln Cavalry Association, 1902.

Bryan, Janet Allan, ed. *A March Past: Reminiscences of Elizabeth Randolph Preston Allan.* Richmond: Dietz Press, 1938.

Craddock, Charles Egbert [Mary N. Murfree]. *In the Tennessee Mountains.* Boston: Houghton, Mifflin, 1884.

Davidson, James Wood. *The Living Writers of the South.* New York: Carleton, 1869.

Du Pont, Henry A. *The Campaign of 1864 in the Valley of Virginia and the Expedition to Lynchburg.* New York: National Americana Society, 1925.

Eby, Cecil D., Jr., ed. *A Virginia Yankee in the Civil War: The Diaries of David Hunter Strother.* Chapel Hill: University of North Carolina Press, 1961.

Exercises at the Unveiling of the Junkin Memorial Tablet, at Lafayette College, Easton, Pa., Tuesday, May 24th, 1887. Easton, Pa.: The College, 1887?.

Hayne, Paul Hamilton. *The Mountain of the Lovers; with Poems of Nature and Tradition.* New York: Hale, 1875.

Junkin, George. *An Address Delivered before the Literary Societies of Rutgers College.* New York: Pruden & Martin, 1856.

———. *"The Integrity of Our National Union, vs. Abolitionism: An Argument from the Bible, in Proof of the Position that Believing Masters Ought to be Honored and Obeyed by Their Own Servants, and Tolerated in, Not Excommunicated from, the Church of God": Being Part of a Speech Delivered Before the Synod of Cincinnati, on the Subject of Slavery, September 19th and 20th, 1843.* Cincinnati: Donogh, 1843.

———. *Political Fallacies: An Examination of the False Assumptions, and Refutation of the Sophistical Reasonings, Which Have Brought on This Civil War.* New York: Scribner, 1863.

———. *A Treatise on Justification.* 2nd ed. Philadelphia: Martin, 1849.

Longfellow, Henry Wadsworth, ed. *Poems of Places.* 31 vols. Boston: Osgood, 1876–79.

May, Caroline. *The American Female Poets: With Biographical and Critical Notices.* Philadelphia: Lindsay & Blakiston, 1848.

Moore, Rayburn S., ed. *A Man of Letters in the Nineteenth-Century South: Selected Letters of Paul Hamilton Hayne.* Baton Rouge: Louisiana State University Press, 1982.

Pickett, La Salle Corbell. *Literary Hearthstones of Dixie.* Philadelphia: Lippincott, 1912.

Preston, G. J. "Alpenglow." *Lippincott's* 35 (June 1885): 606–7.

Read, Thomas Buchanan. *The Female Poets of America. With Portraits, Biographical Notices, and Specimens of Their Writings.* 5th ed. Philadelphia: Butler, 1852.

Review of *Cartoons, Lippincott's* 17 (May 1876): 647.

Review of *Silverwood, Southern Literary Messenger* 24 (January 1857): 80.

Simms, William Gilmore, ed. *War Poetry of the South.* New York: Richardson, 1867.

Tardy, Mary T., ed. *The Living Female Writers of the South.* Philadelphia: Claxton, Remsen & Haffelfinger, 1872; reprint, Detroit: Gale Research, 1978.

Trial of the Rev. Albert Barnes, Before the Synod of Philadelphia, In Session at York, October 1835. On a Charge of Heresy, Preferred against Him by the Rev. Geo. Junkin: With All the Pleadings and Debate. Reported for the *New York Observer* by Arthur J. Stansbury. New York: Van Nostrand & Dwight, 1836.

War Lyrics and Songs of the South. London: Spottiswoode, 1866.

Whittier, John Greenleaf, ed. *Songs of Three Centuries.* Boston: Osgood, 1876.

Williams, Charles Richard, ed. *Diary and Letters of Rutherford Birchard Hayes: Nineteenth President of the United States.* Vol. 2: *1861–1865.* Columbus: Ohio State Archaeological and Historical Society, 1922; reprint, New York: Kraus Reprint, 1971.

Wilson, Clyde N., and Shirley Bright Cook, eds. *The Papers of John C. Calhoun.* Vol. 23: *1846.* Columbia: University of South Carolina Press, 1996.

Secondary Sources

Ahlstrom, Sydney E. *A Religious History of the American People.* New Haven: Yale University Press, 1972.

Arvin, Newton. *Longfellow: His Life and Work.* Boston: Little, Brown, 1962.

Ash, Stephen V. *When the Yankees Came: Conflict and Chaos in the Occupied South, 1861–1865.* Chapel Hill & London: University of North Carolina Press, 1995.

Ballagh, James Curtis. *A History of Slavery in Virginia.* Baltimore: Johns Hopkins Press, 1902; reprint, New York: Johnson Reprint, 1968.

Baym, Nina. *American Women Writers and the Work of History, 1790–1860.* New Brunswick, N.J.: Rutgers University Press, 1995.

———. *Woman's Fiction: A Guide to Novels by and about Women in America, 1820–70.* 2nd ed. Urbana: University of Illinois Press, 1993.

Beringer, Richard E., Herman Hattaway, Archer Jones, and William N. Still, Jr. *Why the South Lost the Civil War.* Athens & London: University of Georgia Press, 1986.

Blair, William. *Virginia's Private War: Feeding Body and Soul in the Confederacy, 1861–1865.* New York & Oxford: Oxford University Press, 1998.

Brice, Marshall Moore. *Conquest of a Valley.* Charlottesville: University Press of Virginia, 1965.

Burke, Colin B. *American Collegiate Populations: A Test of the Traditional View.* New York: New York University Press, 1982.

Catton, Bruce. *The Civil War*. New York: American Heritage Press, 1971.

Clinton, Catherine. *Tara Revisited: Women, War, and the Plantation Legend*. New York: Abbeville Press, 1995.

Clinton and Nina Silber, eds. *Divided Houses: Gender and the Civil War*. New York: Oxford University Press, 1992.

Coulling, Mary Price. *Margaret Junkin Preston: A Biography*. Winston-Salem: Blair, 1993.

Coultrap-McQuin, Susan. *Doing Literary Business: American Women Writers in the Nineteenth Century*. Chapel Hill: University of North Carolina Press, 1990.

Cox, Karen L. *Dixie's Daughters: The United Daughters of the Confederacy and the Preservation of Confederate Culture*. New Perspectives on the History of the South. Gainesville: University Press of Florida, 2003.

Crenshaw, Ollinger. *General Lee's College: The Rise and Growth of Washington and Lee University*. New York: Random House, 1969.

Douglas, Ann. *The Feminization of American Culture*. New York: Knopf, 1977.

Eaton, Clement. *The Waning of the Old South Civilization: 1860–1880s*. Athens: University of Georgia Press, 1968.

Fahs, Alice. *The Imagined Civil War: Popular Literature of the North and South, 1861–1865*. Chapel Hill & London: University of North Carolina Press, 2001.

Faust, Drew Gilpin. *The Creation of Confederate Nationalism: Ideology and Identity in the Civil War South*. Baton Rouge: Louisiana State University Press, 1988.

———. *Mothers of Invention: Women of the Slaveholding South in the American Civil War*. Fred W. Morrison Series in Southern Studies. Chapel Hill & London: University of North Carolina Press, 1996.

Foner, Eric. *Reconstruction: America's Unfinished Revolution*. New York: Harper & Row, 1988.

Foster, Gaines M. *Ghosts of the Confederacy: Defeat, the Lost Cause, and the Emergence of the New South, 1865 to 1913*. New York: Oxford University Press, 1987.

Fox-Genovese, Elizabeth. *Within the Plantation Household: Black and White Women of the Old South*. Gender and American Culture Series. Chapel Hill: University of North Carolina Press, 1988.

French, John C. "Preston, Margaret Junkin." In *Dictionary of American Biography*. Vol. 15, edited by Harris Elwood Starr, 204–5. New York: Scribners, 1935.

Gardner, Sarah E. *Blood and Irony: Southern White Women's Narratives of the Civil War, 1861–1937*. Chapel Hill & London: University of North Carolina Press, 2004.

Geiger, Roger, ed. *The American College in the Nineteenth Century*. Nashville: Vanderbilt University Press, 2000.

Grimsley, Mark. *The Hard Hand of War: Union Military Policy Toward Southern Civilians, 1861–1865*. Cambridge & New York: Cambridge University Press, 1995.

Hatch, Nathan O. *The Democratization of American Christianity*. New Haven: Yale University Press, 1989.

Havighurst, Walter. *The Miami Years: 1809–1969*, 2nd ed. New York: Putnam, 1969.

Heron, John W. "George Junkin, D.D., L.L.D." In *The Diamond Anniversary Volume*, edited by Walter Lawrence Tobey and William Oxley Thompson. Hamilton, Ohio: Republican Publishing, 1899.

Hubbell, Jay B. *The South in American Literature, 1607–1900*. Durham: Duke University Press, 1954.

Isenberg, Nancy, and Andrew Burstein, eds. *Mortal Remains: Death in Early America.* Philadelphia: University of Pennsylvania Press, 2003.

Johannsen, Robert W. *To the Halls of the Montezumas: The Mexican War in the American Imagination.* New York: Oxford University Press, 1985.

———, ed. *Democracy on Trial: A Documentary History of American Life, 1845–1877.* 2nd ed. Urbana: University of Illinois Press, 1988.

Jones, Anne Goodwyn. *Tomorrow Is Another Day: The Woman Writer in the South, 1859–1936.* Baton Rouge & London: Louisiana State University Press, 1981.

Kelley, Mary. *Private Woman, Public Stage: Literary Domesticity in Nineteenth-Century America.* New York: Oxford University Press, 1984.

Kerber, Linda K. *Toward an Intellectual History of Women: Essays.* Chapel Hill: University of North Carolina Press, 1997.

Klein, Stacey Jean. "Wielding the Pen: Margaret Preston, Confederate Nationalistic Literature, and the Expansion of a Woman's Place in the South." *Civil War History* 49 (September 2003): 221–34.

Kraditor, Aileen S. *Means and Ends in American Abolitionism: Garrison and His Critics on Strategy and Tactics, 1834–1850.* New York: Pantheon, 1969.

Laderman, Gary. *The Sacred Remains: American Attitudes toward Death, 1799–1883.* New Haven: Yale University Press, 1997.

Lowe, Richard. "Another Look at Reconstruction in Virginia." *Civil War History* 32 (March 1986): 56–76.

Lystra, Karen. *Searching the Heart: Women, Men, and Romantic Love in Nineteenth-Century America.* New York & Oxford: Oxford University Press, 1989.

Mackethan, Lucinda H. "Plantation Fiction, 1865–1900." In *The History of Southern Literature,* edited by Louis D. Rubin, Jr., Blyden Jackson, Rayburn S. Moore, Lewis P. Simpson, and Thomas Daniel Young, 209–18. Baton Rouge: Louisiana State University Press, 1985.

Maddex, Jack P., Jr. "Proslavery Millennialism: Social Eschatology in Antebellum Southern Calvinism." In *Religion and Slavery,* edited by Paul Finkelman. New York: Garland, 1989.

———. *The Virginia Conservatives, 1867–1879: A Study in Reconstruction Politics.* Chapel Hill: University of North Carolina Press, 1970.

McGreevy, Patrick V. *Imagining Niagara: The Meaning and Making of Niagara Falls.* Amherst: University of Massachusetts Press, 1994.

McKinsey, Elizabeth. *Niagara Falls: Icon of the American Sublime.* Cambridge: Cambridge University Press, 1985.

Miller, Edward A., Jr. *Lincoln's Abolitionist General: The Biography of David Hunter.* Columbia: University of South Carolina Press, 1997.

Moore, Rayburn S. "'Courtesies of the Guild' and More: Paul Hamilton Hayne and Margaret Junkin Preston." *Mississippi Quarterly: The Journal of Southern Culture* 43 (Fall 1990): 485–93.

———. "Introduction to Part II." In *The History of Southern Literature,* edited by Rubin et al., 177.

———. *Paul Hamilton Hayne.* New York: Twayne, 1972.

———. "Poetry of the Late Nineteenth Century." In *The History of Southern Literature,* edited by Rubin et al., 188–98.

Moss, Elizabeth. *Domestic Novelists in the Old South: Defenders of Southern Culture.* Southern Literary Studies Series. Baton Rouge & London: Louisiana State University Press, 1992.

Muhlenfeld, Elisabeth. "The Civil War and Authorship." In *The History of Southern Literature,* edited by Rubin et al., 178–87.

Nye, Russel Blaine. *The Cultural Life of the New Nation: 1776–1830.* New York: Harper & Row, 1960.

———. *Society and Culture in America: 1830–1860.* New York: Harper & Row, 1974.

O'Brien, Michael. *Conjectures of Order: Intellectual Life and the American South, 1810–1860.* Chapel Hill & London: University of North Carolina Press, 2004.

Orians, G. Harrison. "The Rise of Romanticism, 1805–1855." In *Transitions in American Literary History,* edited by Harry Hayden Clark, 163–244. Durham: Duke University Press, 1953.

Pease, Jane H., and William H. Pease. *Ladies, Women, and Wenches: Choice and Constraint in Antebellum Charleston and Boston.* Gender and American Culture Series. Chapel Hill & London: University of North Carolina Press, 1990.

Phillips, Edward H. *The Shenandoah Valley in 1864: An Episode in the History of Warfare.* Monograph Series. Charleston: The Citadel, 1965.

Potter, David M. *The Impending Crisis: 1848–1861,* edited by Don E. Fehrenbacher. New York: Harper & Row, 1976.

Potts, David B. *Baptist Colleges in the Development of American Society, 1812–1861.* New York: Garland, 1988.

Rable, George C. *Civil Wars: Women and the Crisis of Southern Nationalism.* Women in American History Series. Urbana & Chicago: University of Illinois Press, 1989.

Robertson, James I., Jr. *Stonewall Jackson: The Man, The Soldier, The Legend.* New York: Macmillan, 1997.

Rothman, Ellen K. *Hands and Hearts: A History of Courtship in America.* New York: Basic Books, 1984.

Rubin, Louis D., Jr. *The Edge of the Swamp: A Study in the Literature and Society of the Old South.* Baton Rouge: Louisiana State University Press, 1989.

Rubin, Louis D., Jr., Blyden Jackson, Rayburn S. Moore, Lewis P. Simpson, and Thomas Daniel Young, eds. *The History of Southern Literature.* Baton Rouge: Louisiana State University Press, 1985.

Saum, Lewis O. "Death in the Popular Mind of Pre–Civil War America." *American Quarterly* 26 (December 1974): 477–95.

Scott, Anne Firor. *Natural Allies: Women's Associations in American History.* Urbana: University of Illinois Press, 1991.

Skaggs, Merrill Maguire. "Varieties of Local Color." In *The History of Southern Literature,* edited by Rubin et al., 219–27.

Skillman, David Bishop. *The Biography of a College: Being the History of the First Century of the Life of Lafayette College.* Vol. 1: *1824–1879.* Easton, Pa.: Lafayette College, 1932.

Spencer, Benjamin T. *The Quest for Nationality: An American Literary Campaign.* Syracuse: Syracuse University Press, 1957.

Spencer, Donald S. *Louis Kossuth and Young America: A Study of Sectionalism and Foreign Policy, 1848–1852.* Columbia: University of Missouri Press, 1977.

Starr, Harris Elwood. "Junkin, George." In *Dictionary of American Biography*. Vol. 10, edited by Dumas Malone, 248–49. New York: Scribners, 1933.

Staudenraus, P. J. *The African Colonization Movement, 1816–1865*. New York: Columbia University Press, 1961.

Tobias, Marilyn. *Old Dartmouth on Trial: The Transformation of the Academic Community in Nineteenth-Century America*. New York & London: New York University Press, 1982.

Upham, A. H. *The Centennial of Miami University*. Ohio Archaeological and Historical Society Quarterly; reprint, Columbus, Ohio: Fred J. Heer, 1909.

INDEX

Note: Authors' names are given as they were at the time of publication or composition.

Portland Community College